DR. GARY SMALLEY
TED CUNNINGHAM

STUDY GUIDE

The Language of Sex

experiencing the beauty
of sexual intimacy

Regal

From Gospel Light
Ventura, California, U.S.A.

Published by Regal
From Gospel Light
Ventura, California, U.S.A.
www.regalbooks.com
Printed in the U.S.A.

Library of Congress Cataloging-in-Publication Data
Smalley, Gary.
  The language of sex study guide / Gary Smalley and Ted Cunningham.
    p. cm.
  ISBN 978-0-8307-4610-1 (trade paper)
  1. Sex—Religious aspects—Christianity. I. Cunningham, Ted. II. Title.
  BT708.S626 2008
  261.8'357—dc22
                                                                      2007044028

1 2 3 4 5 6 7 8 9 10 / ·10 09 08

Rights for publishing this book outside the U.S.A. or in non-English languages are administered by Gospel Light Worldwide, an international not-for-profit ministry. For additional information, please visit www.glww.org, email info@glww.org, or write to Gospel Light Worldwide, 1957 Eastman Avenue, Ventura, CA 93003, U.S.A.

Contents

Introduction

The Language of Sex Study Guide is designed to be used in conjunction with *The Language of Sex* book and DVD. Whether you enjoy the study with your spouse, in a small group or as part of a church seminar, we encourage you to share what you're learning with those closest to you! Talk about the questions and Scriptures with your spouse, friends and mentors. As you grow closer to God and your spouse over the course of the study, don't be shy about sharing the good news of what God is doing in your life.

Each section begins with an introduction, followed by some open-ended questions, "For Starters," which are designed to get the discussion going. After you complete that section, you'll want to watch the DVD to see Gary and Ted share their thoughts and insights on the material. Then it's time for "Discussion and Study," the main section of each session. You'll want to keep your Bible nearby. There are lots of great Scriptures and questions to reflect on and discuss. Next there will be an easy-to-remember summary called "Taking It with You" to help you internalize what you've learned, and last you'll have the opportunity to put these lessons into practice before the next session by selecting at least one of three options from "Putting It into Practice."

Our hope and prayer for you is that God will use this study to awaken your heart for Him and for your spouse. And that you'll discover the marriage you never thought possible!

The Foundations of Honor and Security

Chapters 1–3 in *The Language of Sex*

Several years ago, the pastors of our church were meeting at Panera Bread to brainstorm and plan the Song of Songs series we were going to start on the following Sunday morning. We were having a blast and being quite graphic as we followed the text, having more fun than you could possibly imagine with Solomon. We were laughing and quoting and so on. One of our pastors got up to get a refill and met a guy at the coffee center.

The guy asked, "What do you guys do for a living?"

"We are pastors," one of my friends replied.

"What church?" the guy asked.

"Woodland Hills," I responded.

"Sounds like my kind of church!" the guy responded.

For way too long, the Church has been silent on the issue of sexual intimacy. As a result, many Christians and non-Christians have developed an unhealthy understanding of one of God's greatest gifts: sex.

That's why in the upcoming study, we're going to give you the tools you need to enjoy the best sex of your life, as well as the marriage you've always hoped for!

Now the key to the best possible sex and marriage is found in the following equation:

Honor ➝ Security ➝ Intimacy ➝ *Sex*

What does this equation have to do with the best sex of your life? Honor creates security. Security creates intimacy. And intimacy sets the stage for great sex. The truth is that you cannot have great sex—let alone a healthy relationship—without honor and security.

In this session, we're going to explore the issues of honor and security and the vital role they play in your marriage and sex life.

For Starters

When you think of the word "honor," what comes to mind?

_____

_____

_____

_____

_____

_____

_____

_____

_____

In what practical ways do you honor your spouse?

_____

_____

_____

_____

_____

_____

_____

_____

_____

What are the ways your spouse feels most honored? Are there any differences between the ways you think your spouse feels most honored and the ways your spouse actually feels honored? If so, explain.

_____

_____

_____

_____

_____

_____

_____

_____

_____

_____

Introduction to DVD

The foundation for every great marriage begins with honor and security. In this first session, we'll discover how these issues are foundational not only to the best possible marriage but also to the best possible sex life. Let's watch as Gary and Ted introduce this idea.

Discussion and Study

Honor is the foundation of every great relationship, including our relationship with God. We are called and created to honor God. In the following verses, in what way is honor displayed to God?

Psalm 29:2

_____

_____

_____

_____

_____

_____

_____

_____

_____

_____

Psalm 107:32

_____

_____

_____

_____

_____

_____

_____

_____

_____

Isaiah 25:1

_____

_____

_____

_____

_____

_____

_____

_____

_____

List five specific ways in which you honor God in your own life.

1. _____

2. _____

3. _____

4. _____

5. _____

While God is the One who deserves all honor and glory, we are also meant to honor one another by loving each other. Jesus said that the greatest commandments are to love God with everything we've got and to love our neighbors as ourselves. That includes honoring one another. The word "honor" means attaching high value to someone or something. When we honor something or someone, a feeling often wells up inside of us and affects our actions and attitudes. We may feel gratitude or a sense of joy when we think about the other person.

Now honoring isn't just something we do to our bosses, coworkers or friends. It's meant to be something we do regularly in our marriages.

I (Gary) discovered this early on in my marriage to Norma, when after a heated discussion I realized that the way I was living my life communicated that almost anything and everything were more important to me than she was. I was undermining my relationship with my wife without even realizing it, because I didn't honor her. It all goes back to that equation:

HONOR → Security → Intimacy → *Sex*

Take a second look at the Scriptures that prescribe honor to God. As you reflect on the verses below, what insights do you have on how you can honor your spouse?

Psalm 29:2

_____
_____
_____
_____
_____
_____
_____
_____

Psalm 107:32

_____
_____
_____
_____
_____
_____
_____
_____

Isaiah 25:1

_____
_____
_____

_____
_____
_____
_____
_____
_____
_____
_____

What many people don't realize is that honoring someone else is really a heart issue. If we don't honor ourselves, then it's going to be harder to honor someone else. If we are extra critical or hard on ourselves, then we'll probably have the same attitude toward others—including our spouse!

Take a look at the following statements. Write your name next to those that you sometimes say to yourself. Write your spouse's name next to those that he or she sometimes says to him- or herself.

I'm such a dummy. _____
I'm such an idiot. _____
I'm an airhead. _____
I'll never get it right. _____
I'm so slow. _____
I'll never amount to anything. _____
I'm such a loser. _____
No one likes me. _____
Duh! _____

It's amazing how hard we can be on ourselves without even realizing it! If you or your spouse's name appears more than once on this list, it's a good time to take a moment and pray. Ask God to change your hearts—that you would be a source of encouragement and life to one another. Ask God to forgive you for being so hard on yourself, and ask Him to reveal the depths of His love for you!

Honoring Your Marriage

Honoring your spouse means honoring your marriage and recognizing that not only is your spouse a gift from God, so is the institution of marriage.

Read Genesis 2:18. Notice that God didn't just make "a helper" but "a helper suitable for him." Why do you think God took so much care in His design of a spouse for Adam?

_____

_____

_____

_____

_____

_____

_____

_____

The word for "helper" in Genesis 2:18 is *ezer*, which means "one who helps." It refers to someone who comes alongside to offer assistance, and it's the same word that refers to God in the following verses. Look up the following Scriptures and write each one below its reference.

Psalm 33:20

_____

_____

_____

_____

_____

_____

_____

Psalm 70:1

_____

_____

_____

_____
_____
_____

Psalm 115:9

_____
_____
_____
_____
_____
_____
_____

_____

God gave you your spouse to come alongside you to give you assistance. He did not give you your spouse as a replacement for Himself. You honor God when you honor your marriage.

"The two most important principles that keep a couple in love and in a mutually satisfying relationship: (1) Honor your spouse and (2) keep your relationship secure" (p. 27 in *The Language of Sex*).

Building Security in Your Marriage

One of the best ways to build security is to pour your energy into honoring your spouse and looking for opportunities to meet and nurture your spouse's desires. When you create security in your relationship, the temperature of your love life will go up.

Honor ⟶ **SECURITY** ⟶ Intimacy ⟶ *Sex*

So how do you build security in your marriage? One of the best ways is to guard your spouse's heart. That means whenever conflict arises, you need to take care of it right away.

Guard Your Spouse's Heart

"Sex is only a barometer of the marriage. Honor leads to security, security leads to intimacy and intimacy leads to sex. Security means building honor into your relationship and esteeming your mate as highly valuable. Security means seeing your mate as personally autographed by God. When you grow the security within your marriage, the natural fruit is intimacy" (p. 39).

Read Song of Songs 2:14-15 and write the verses below.

_____

_____

_____

_____

_____

_____

"In Song of Songs 2:15, Solomon's girlfriend says, 'Catch for us the foxes.' While that can be interpreted many ways, I think it points to the 'foxes' of conflict that run through all of our lives. In essence, she's saying, 'When conflict arises let's take care of it right away.' When you take care of the 'foxes,' you create security, and intimacy naturally grows" (p. 44).

What foxes are running through your relationship with your spouse right now? Are there any foxes that you need to catch and remove from your marriage?

_____

_____

_____

_____

_____

_____

Commit 100 Percent to the Marriage

God's plan for your marriage is that you spend your entire lifetime learning and growing together. Maybe that's one reason why Malachi says that God hates divorce. It's not the divorced person that God hates, but the breaking of the bonds that naturally happen in marriage. While those who have gone through a divorce can experience grace, freedom, forgiveness and restoration from the Lord, divorce is against God's best plan for each person's life.

Read Malachi 2:10-16. Why do you think God is so opposed to divorce?

_____

_____

_____

_____

_____

_____

Marriage is representative of something greater than just the union between a man and a woman. It's also representative of God's relationship with His people, the Church. According to the passages below, what can we learn about God's desire for a relationship with us?

Isaiah 62:5

_____

_____

_____

_____

_____

_____

2 Corinthians 11:2

_____

_____

_____

_____

_____

_____

Revelation 19:7

_____

_____

_____

_____

_____

_____

_____

Revelation 21:2

_____

_____

_____

_____

_____

_____

In these verses, God's tremendous love is revealed to us. It's not just a verbal commitment but part of a covenant—an irrevocable promise from God that He is committed to fulfilling His purposes and promises. When we verbally remind our spouses that we're committed no matter what, we don't just increase honor in our marriages, but we also provide security to our spouses. Secure in that love, the relationship can't help but blossom and grow.

Develop Healthy Boundaries

Ephesians 5:31 says, "For this cause shall a man leave his father and mother, and shall cleave to his wife; and the two shall become one flesh" (*ASV*). That word for "cleave" is translated as "glue" in modern Hebrew. A married man and woman are designed to become glue, but that natural bond cannot form if they are still cleaving to Mom, Dad, old dating relationships or addictions.

Reflecting on your own marriage, are there any unhealthy boundaries that are undermining your relationship?

_____

_____

_____

_____

_____

Taking It with You

Honor and security are crucial to strengthening your marriage!

HONOR ➝ **SECURITY** ➝ Intimacy ➝ *Sex*

Honor and security naturally lead to intimacy in a relationship. In the next session, you'll discover some of the differences between men and women and how you can begin celebrating those differences in your own marriage and growth toward intimacy. To prepare for the next session, read chapters 4 through 6 in *The Language of Sex*.

Putting It into Practice

Choose at least one of these suggested activities to complete over the next week. Consider sharing with your friends or small-group members the impact it has on you and your relationship with your spouse.

1. Honor Your Spouse Through Scripture
One of the best ways you can honor your spouse is by recognizing your mate's incredible worth. One of the ways to do this is by using

Scripture. In the following verses, read your spouse's name in place of each blank line:

> For You created _____'s inmost being; You knit _____ together in _____'s mother's womb. I praise You because _____ is fearfully and wonderfully made; Your works are wonderful, I know that full well. _____'s frame was not hidden from You when _____ was made in the secret place. When _____ was woven together in the depths of the earth, Your eyes saw _____'s unformed body. All the days ordained for _____ were written in Your book before one of them came to be (see Psalm 139:13-16).

Now look up the following Scriptures in your Bible and read them aloud to your spouse:

- Isaiah 43:1-7 (substitute "God" for "I" and "His" for "my")

- Romans 8:38-39 (substitute your spouse's name for "us")

- 1 Corinthians 13

- Ephesians 3:17-19

2. Honor Your Love with Confirmation Bias

You can build honor and security in your marriage through a breakthrough concept called confirmation bias. Here's the secret: When you make a decision about someone, your feelings follow. People tend to only see what they believe. So if you believe your spouse is worthless, incompetent or always late, then you will only see and recognize the behaviors that support that belief.

Philippians 4:8 says, "Whatever is true, whatever is noble, whatever is right, whatever is pure, whatever is lovely, whatever is admirable—if anything is excellent or praiseworthy—think about such things." In the space below, write the ways in which your spouse fulfills each description.

True

_____

_____

_____

_____

_____

Noble

_____

_____

_____

_____

_____

Right

_____

_____

_____

_____

_____

Pure

_____

_____

_____

_____

_____

Lovely

_____

_____

_____

_____

Admirable

_____
_____
_____
_____
_____
_____

Excellent

_____
_____
_____
_____
_____
_____

Praiseworthy

_____
_____
_____
_____
_____
_____

Over the next week, commit to praying for your spouse in each of these areas. Ask God to reveal to you ways in which you may not even have realized that your spouse is true, noble, right, pure, lovely, admirable, excellent and praiseworthy. At the end of the week, share your list with your spouse.

You'll be amazed at how your attitude and relationship will change! That's the secret of confirmation bias and it bears repeating: When you make a decision about someone, your feelings follow. So go ahead and make the best decisions possible about your spouse.

3. Practice the Five-Minute Rule

The Bible challenges us in our relationships to "be completely humble and gentle; bearing with one another in love" (Ephesians 4:2). So now I (Ted) use the Five-Minute Rule: When I encounter conflict that isn't easily resolved, I put myself in a time-out.

Following the instruction of James 1:19 to "be quick to listen, slow to speak and slow to become angry," I go away for at least five minutes and ask God to help me open my heart back up. During this time, I refuse to sulk, pout, whine, complain or even come up with three reasons why it's her fault. I take 100 percent responsibility for my heart. And every time I do, the bond of our love, respect and security is not only preserved but also nurtured.

Let your spouse know that you are committed to practicing the Five-Minute Rule when you encounter a conflict that isn't easily resolved. Ask your spouse to hold you accountable. If a discussion gets heated, give your spouse full permission to gently remind you to put yourself in a time-out. Use the five minutes to pray and ask for God's perspective and heart on the matter. Ask God to change *you*—not your spouse.

The Five-Minute Rule helps our hearts stay open to each other. And when the heart is open, every door is open: to great conversations, time together, intimacy and sex.

Celebrate Differences and Discover Communication

Chapters 4-6 in *The Language of Sex*

Sometimes I (Ted) think there are too many differences between men and women to count! We see them in different situations every day. We even see them in children.

I recently attended a YMCA preschooler basketball game. Each team had five members on the court, consisting of four boys and one girl. As I looked out on the court, I noticed the two girls—from opposing teams—standing near the sidelines, chatting away. Meanwhile, the eight guys were busy fighting for the ball. The girls wanted to talk, build relationship and connect—it didn't matter that it was game time. But the guys wanted to play ball and win.

I smiled whenever the ball would get stolen during the game. The guys on the teams would thunder down the court, but the girls seemed unaffected—they just kept chatting! The coach would yell, "They're down there now!" And the girls would jog down to the other side of the court, conversation still in play.

It's not just on the basketball court that we see differences. Recently, some friends came over to our house to watch a game. When the chip bowl emptied, the competition among the guys was on.

Someone commented, "Hey, no more chips in the bowl."

"Yeah," someone agreed.

"You go get more chips," someone suggested.

"No, you—after all, I bought them."

The issue wasn't the chips at all, but the competition to decide who would give in and actually fill the bowl.

When a snack bowl empties at a women's event, they usually respond a little differently. They get up as a group—at least two, if not all of them—make their way to the kitchen and refill the bowl, talking the entire time. Then they come back, sit down and continue the situation.

The tendencies of the sexes are obviously different.

And those differences are beautiful in God's eyes. God looks at the differences between all of us and finds joy because He made us and created us. He has given each of us a unique blend of gifts, talents, strengths and weaknesses.

In this session, we're going to learn to celebrate those differences! We'll also look at how to take communication to the next level so that you can foster intimacy in your marriage relationship.

For Starters

In the space below, list three ways that you and your spouse are alike. These can include gifts, talents, weaknesses, interests, passions, visions, dreams and hopes.

1. _____

2. _____

3. _____

Now list three ways that you and your spouse are different.

1. _____

2. _____

3. _____

In what ways do those differences complement each other? In what ways do those differences help add balance to each of your lives?

_____

_____

_____

_____

_____

Introduction to DVD

As we've discovered, the foundation for every great marriage begins with honor and security. One of the best ways to build honor and security in your marriage is to learn to appreciate the differences between you and your spouse. When you begin celebrating differences in your marriage, you create intimacy. In this second session, you'll discover some of the common differences between men and women as well as how to improve your communication. Let's watch as Gary introduces these ideas.

Discussion and Study

Intimacy has often been explained as "into-me-see." It's a relationship of knowing and being known. More than anyone, God desires an intimate relationship with you. Not only does God know you, but He also wants to be known by you. Psalm 139 is an incredible passage that describes how because God made us, He knows things about us that we don't even know about ourselves!

Read Psalm 139:14-18. Make a list of all the things God has done for us and knows about us.

_____

_____

_____

_____

_____

God doesn't just know everything about us—He wants us to know Him. In the passages below, what promises are given to those who seek God, who desire an intimate relationship with Him?

Deuteronomy 4:29

_____
_____
_____
_____
_____
_____
_____
_____
_____

2 Chronicles 7:14

_____
_____
_____
_____
_____
_____
_____
_____

Psalm 9:10

_____
_____
_____
_____
_____

_____

_____

_____

These Scriptures suggest that there are great rewards for those who seek God. Just as we are created to know and be known by God in an intimate relationship, we are also to have an intimate relationship with our spouse.

When you reflect on your marriage relationship so far, how have you seen your level of intimacy with your spouse increase?

_____

_____

_____

_____

_____

_____

_____

_____

On a scale of 1 to 10, how much do you feel that you know about your spouse?

| 1 | 2 | 3 | 4 | 5 | 6 | 7 | 8 | 9 | 10 |

Nothing   Everything

On a scale of 1 to 10, how much do you feel that your spouse knows about you?

| 1 | 2 | 3 | 4 | 5 | 6 | 7 | 8 | 9 | 10 |

Nothing   Everything

What kinds of activities tend to build intimacy in your marriage?

_____

_____

_____

_____

_____

_____

_____

_____

What kinds of activities tend to undermine intimacy in your marriage?

_____

_____

_____

_____

_____

_____

_____

_____

Discovering true intimacy begins with understanding and celebrating the unique differences made by God between men and women. Intimacy does not begin in the bedroom. Intimacy begins with honor and security—as we explored in the first session—and results in sex—as we'll discover in the next session.

Honor ➛ Security ➛ **INTIMACY** ➛ *Sex*

"Intimacy includes the everyday acts of kindness, consistency and communication that build longing and eventually create a desire for sex in women. The best sex of your life begins with what some might consider nonsexual contact—holding hands, touching shoulders, a warm hug" (p. 52).

When we discover the differences between men and women in a healthy way, then we are better equipped to honor those differences. They enable us to offer understanding, compassion and forgiveness. They offer an antidote for negative beliefs and assumptions. And they can even help increase the curiosity, fascination and intrigue in marriage!

For each pair in the quiz below, circle which characteristic most describes you.

QUICK BRAIN QUIZ

a. Visual`	b. Verbal
a. Spatial	b. Linguistic
a. Big picture	b. Details
a. Emotional	b. Practical
a. Abstract	b. Concrete
a. Shapes and patterns	b. Orderly sequences

If most of your answers are *a*, you tend to favor the right side of your brain. If most of your answers are *b*, you tend to favor the left side of your brain.

Now here's what is interesting: 80 percent of men tend to favor the left side of the brain. That's the side that includes the logic and language systems. It's the part of the brain that excels at things like engineering and accounting.

Meanwhile, 80 percent of women tend to favor the right side of the brain. This side is highly creative and excels at things like art and design.[1]

Whether you're right-brained or left-brained, you have a lot of strengths and gifts that you bring to your marriage.

How does your spouse's response to this quiz differ from your own? In what areas do you tend to think alike?

_____

_____

_____

_____

_____

_____

_____

"Did you know that the human brain is so fabulous and powerful that the average person only uses 8 percent of the brain's mental capacity? That means that we all have the ability to grow and change in our cognitive abilities and relational skills. If you tend to favor the left or right side of your brain, you can learn to use the other side! Every man and woman has tremendous potential!" (p. 66).

The Five Key Differences that Build Security

Chapter 4 in *The Language of Sex* highlights the five key differences between men and women. Take a look at each difference, circle your place on the scale and then respond to the corresponding questions.

1. Men tend to discover and express facts, while women tend to express intuition and their emotions.

1	2	3	4	5	6	7	8	9	10

Strongly disagree   Strongly agree

Do you agree or disagree that this statement is true in your marriage? Explain.

_____

_____

_____

_____

_____
_____
_____
_____
_____

How can you make this an area of greater agreement and appreciation between you and your spouse?

_____
_____
_____
_____
_____
_____
_____
_____
_____

2. Men tend to look for solutions, while women tend to look for compassion, empathy and understanding.

1	2	3	4	5	6	7	8	9	10

Strongly disagree   Strongly agree

Do you agree or disagree that this statement is true in your marriage? Explain.

_____
_____
_____
_____
_____
_____

How can you make this an area of greater agreement and appreciation between you and your spouse?

_____

_____

_____

_____

_____

_____

_____

_____

3. Men tend to be objective, while women tend to be personal.

1	2	3	4	5	6	7	8	9	10

Strongly disagree   Strongly agree

Do you agree or disagree that this statement is true in your marriage? Explain.

_____

_____

_____

_____

_____

_____

_____

_____

_____

How can you make this an area of greater agreement and appreciation between you and your spouse?

_____

_____

_____

_____
_____
_____
_____
_____
_____

4. A lot of men can separate who they are from their surroundings, but the home is an extension of most women.

| 1 | 2 | 3 | 4 | 5 | 6 | 7 | 8 | 9 | 10 |

Strongly disagree   Strongly agree

Do you agree or disagree that this statement is true in your marriage? Explain.

_____
_____
_____
_____
_____
_____
_____
_____

How can you make this an area of greater agreement and appreciation between you and your spouse?

_____
_____
_____
_____
_____
_____

5. Men tend to focus on the basics, while women tend to focus on details that make up the big picture.

1	2	3	4	5	6	7	8	9	10

Strongly disagree   Strongly agree

Do you agree or disagree that this statement is true in your marriage? Explain.

_____

_____

_____

_____

_____

_____

_____

_____

How can you make this an area of greater agreement and appreciation between you and your spouse?

_____

_____

_____

_____

_____

_____

_____

_____

One of the ways to celebrate the differences—not just in your own marriage but in all of your relationships—is to realize that God made every person unique for His purposes. Peter and Paul were very different in their personalities, yet both were used mightily by God.

Read Matthew 14:22-31, Matthew 26:69-75 and John 6:60-69. Reflecting on these passages, how would you describe Peter? How was God able to use Peter?

_____

_____

_____

_____

_____

_____

_____

Read Acts 16:36-37; 20:25-37 and 2 Timothy 4:7-8. Reflecting on these passages, how would you describe Paul? How was God able to use Paul?

_____

_____

_____

_____

_____

_____

_____

Though Peter and Paul were very different, God used both of them to build the Church and lead many into a relationship with Jesus. Our differences—the areas where we are unique—can become areas of great strength, blessing and encouragement when we use them to glorify God.

Setting the Stage for the Best Communication

In addition to celebrating differences, communication is also crucial to developing honor, security and intimacy in a marriage. In fact, good communication can improve all of our relationships!

"Great sex begins with taking the time to first listen to your mate and understand as many things about them as you can. Listening is honoring. Listening is security, especially when you don't react, but instead become genuinely curious and fascinated by what your mate is saying to you" (p. 76).

You may not realize just how important your words are in your marriage and other relationships. Read Proverbs 18:21. Just how much power is there in your words?

_____

_____

_____

_____

_____

_____

_____

During the past week, who have you spoken words of life to? What was the result?

Name or Initials of Person Result

During the past week, who have you spoken words of death to? What was the result?

Name or Initials of Person Result

_____   _____
_____   _____
_____   _____
_____   _____

The Bible provides practical and valuable insight on how to develop strong communication skills. Look up the passages below. What can you learn from the following Scriptures to enhance your communication skills?

Exodus 20:16

_____
_____
_____
_____
_____
_____

Proverbs 15:28

_____
_____
_____
_____
_____
_____

Proverbs 16:32

_____
_____
_____
_____
_____
_____

Proverbs 18:13

_____
_____
_____
_____
_____
_____
_____

Matthew 5:33-37

_____
_____
_____
_____
_____
_____

1 Corinthians 13:1

_____
_____
_____
_____
_____
_____

How does miscommunication undermine your relationships? What is the cost to others—God, family, friends and coworkers—when you don't communicate or listen well?

_____
_____
_____
_____

_____

_____

_____

_____

_____

How does learning how to communicate well improve your relationships? Your marriage?

_____

_____

_____

_____

_____

_____

_____

_____

Taking It with You

By learning to celebrate your differences and to communicate effectively, you create an environment where honor and security abound in your marriage. This leads to greater intimacy.

Honor ➝ Security ➝ **INTIMACY** ➝ *Sex*

One of the natural outcomes of growing intimacy in your marriage is great sex. In the next session, you'll discover how to set the stage for the best sex of your life, what the three big sexpectations are, and how to cultivate creativity in your sex life. To prepare for the next session, read chapters 7 through 9 in *The Language of Sex*.

Putting It into Practice

Choose at least one of these suggested activities to complete over the next week. Consider sharing with your friends or small-group members the impact it has on you and your relationship with your spouse.

1. Take the Brain Sex Test

"The Brain Sex Test" is on pages 57-59 of *The Language of Sex*. Take the test separately from your spouse and then compare answers.

Did anything surprise you about your responses to the test?

_____

_____

_____

_____

_____

_____

_____

Did anything surprise you about your spouse's responses?

_____

_____

_____

_____

_____

_____

_____

How did taking the Brain Sex Test help you better understand yourself? Your spouse?

_____

_____

_____

_____

_____

_____

_____

_____

_____

2. The Marriage Manual Checkup

Every woman has a built-in marriage manual. That's the phrase we use to describe the innate desire every woman has for a great relationship. One of the ways you can find out how your marriage is going is to ask each other the following three big questions. Each person should feel comfortable sharing honestly, knowing the responses are designed to help improve and strengthen your relationship.

1. On a scale of 1 to 10, what kind of marriage do you want?

2. On a scale of 1 to 10, where is our marriage today?

3. What would it take today or in the next few weeks to move our relationship to a 10?

3. Jazz Up the Way You Say "I Love You"

Emotional word pictures are a powerful way to help you communicate what you're really thinking and feeling. While they can feel awkward or strange to use at first, when you begin drawing pictures with your words, you can express those things that you just can't seem to find the right words for!

During the upcoming week, try to think of an emotional word picture to describe your love, affection or appreciation for your spouse every day. Let your spouse know of your commitment, and spend some time thinking about the words you want to use. Though simple, this kind of verbal affirmation can breathe new life and fun into your marriage.

Note
1. Anne Moir and David Jessel, *Brain Sex: The Real Difference Between Men and Women* (New York: A Delta Book/Dell Publishing Group, 1989), p. 40.

Foreplay, Intercourse and Creativity

Chapters 7–9 in *The Language of Sex*

God's genius is demonstrated in how He brings two people together to make them one flesh. It's wonderful! It's a mystery! It's beauty! The fact that I (Ted) can take all of my emotions, my heart and the way that I feel toward my wife that I can't always express with words and express them through touch and the physical act of sex is amazing. God's design is simply brilliant! Sex is a gift not only to be enjoyed for consummation and procreation but also for recreation for a husband and wife.

But sometimes in our marriage, we lose the fascination and curiosity that launched us into love. Odds are that when you were first dating, you wanted to know everything you possibly could about the other person. Nothing could keep you apart. As the years of marriage went by, however, you may have found that some of that excitement faded. You may have stopped asking each other great questions. Or you may have stopped taking the time to really communicate. You may have lost some of the emotional curiosity and fascination that initially drew you together. The intimacy in your relationship has been undermined. And over time, the frequency of sex in your marriage has decreased.

Here's the good news: You don't have to let the love in your relationship die. You can keep asking each other great questions. You can keep cultivating a relationship of creativity, spontaneity and fascination.

Your relationship doesn't have to be centered on duty and responsibility. It can be centered on celebrating each other and building a foundation of honor and security that leads to intimacy and great sex.

I love it when I hear older couples say that the sex just keeps getting better and better. In fact, that's not just a good idea—it's a biblical principle. Proverbs 5:18-19 says, "May your fountain be blessed, and may you rejoice in the wife of your youth. A loving doe, a graceful deer—may her breasts satisfy you always, may you ever be captivated by her love."

God's plan for your marriage is that you're not just satisfied by your spouse but that you're also captivated by your spouse. That means that you don't have to lose the fascination and curiosity with time—you can cultivate it and find yourself falling in love all over again.

Remember, the key to the best possible sex and marriage is found in the following equation:

Honor ⟶ Security ⟶ Intimacy ⟶ *Sex*

Honor creates security. Security creates intimacy. And intimacy sets the stage for great sex. In this session, we're going to explore the issues of verbal affirmation, healthy expectations and the cultivation of creativity.

For Starters

How has the romance in your relationship changed since you were first married?

_____

_____

_____

_____

_____

_____

_____

_____

What kinds of activities, words or interactions cultivate romance, affection and fascination in your relationship?

_____

_____

_____

_____

_____

_____

_____

What prevents you from pursuing those activities, exchanging those words and enjoying those interactions more often?

_____

_____

_____

_____

_____

_____

_____

Introduction to DVD

A great marriage is founded on honor and security. When spouses learn to celebrate their differences and discover how to communicate effectively, they naturally cultivate an atmosphere of intimacy, which results in great sex. In this third session, we'll discover how these issues are foundational, not only to the best possible marriage, but also to the best possible sex life. Let's watch as Ted introduces this idea.

Discussion and Study

Great sex begins long before you ever step into the bedroom. The best foreplay starts in the morning by letting your spouse know that he or she is honored and appreciated. That means that it's worthwhile, especially for men, to get up early to simply be together. Personal care, such as taking a shower, shaving and brushing your teeth, communicate that you want to be pleasant to be around. Acts of service, such as taking care of the kids, cleaning and helping with chores without being asked, communicate a willingness to serve. And verbal expressions of love and affection can make your spouse feel honored, loved and even more connected to you.

List five nonsexual activities that help prepare you or make you desire sex with your spouse.

1. _____

2. _____

3. _____

4. _____

5. _____

Verbal affirmation is so important in any relationship. When we affirm each other verbally, we change our perspective on life and ourselves. In the following passages, what verbal affirmation did God offer Joshua?

Joshua 1:6

_____

_____

_____

_____

_____

Joshua 1:7

_____
_____
_____
_____
_____
_____
_____

Joshua 1:9

_____
_____
_____
_____
_____
_____
_____

Joshua 1:18

_____
_____
_____
_____
_____
_____
_____

Why do you think Joshua needed to hear the verbal affirmation more than once?

_____
_____
_____
_____
_____
_____

If Joshua needed to hear verbal affirmation from God multiple times, how much more do you and your spouse need verbal affirmation?

_____

_____

_____

_____

_____

_____

Why do you think it's so important to affirm each other verbally before and after intercourse?

_____

_____

_____

_____

_____

_____

"We've already learned that women are all-day lovers. The emotional connection needs to start early in the morning, and nonsexual touches need to be delivered throughout the day. Lovingly listening to each other while together; helping with the kids, housework and various chores; learning new things together: These and a host of other activities prepare a woman for sex. Distractions must be removed. Domestic support needs to be provided. The bedroom must be prepared" (p. 137).

"The top thing a woman wants from a man is _gentleness_. The top thing a man wants from a woman is _responsiveness_" (p. 111). In what ways do you agree with this statement? In what ways do you disagree?

_____

_____

_____

_____

_____

All of us have insecurities. What are some of the more intimate insecurities that you have when it comes to sex? Share your response with your spouse.

_____

_____

_____

_____

_____

_____

The Three Sexpectations
The Frequency Sexpectation (how often you'll have sex)
The Endurance Sexpectation (how long lovemaking will last)
The Performance Sexpectation (how your lover will perform)

For most people, expectations go a lot further than the bedroom. You may have expectations about your life, your future or your personal growth. You may place expectations that you may not even be aware of on yourself, your spouse or your friends.

In the space below, list the expectations you have for yourself.

_____

_____

_____

_____

_____

_____

In the space below, list the expectations you have for your spouse.

_____

_____

_____

_____

_____

_____

Are your expectations realistic and healthy? Take a moment and pray. Ask God if there are any changes that you need to make in your expectations. List the necessary changes.

_____
_____
_____
_____
_____
_____
_____
_____
_____
_____

"When our experience is close to what we anticipated, we're stronger and more content. That bolsters our ability to keep on loving. But unless we talk about those things and bring our expectations to the surface, our wishes won't be known for sure, and we may find ourselves facing an energy-sapping gap between our desires and our reality" (p. 127).

While expectations can be healthy, they can become unhealthy when we allow them or our response to them to control us. When there's a gap between what we expect and what we get, we can often experience frustration and disappointment. But we also have the opportunity to experience grace and extend it to others!

In what ways are grace and redemption demonstrated in the following?

Proverbs 4:18

_____
_____
_____
_____
_____
_____

2 Corinthians 3:18

_____
_____
_____
_____
_____

2 Thessalonians 1:3

_____
_____
_____
_____
_____

As Christians, we are called by God to be content in all circumstances. We are to find our joy and satisfaction in the One who will not leave us or forsake us. What do the following verses prescribe for a contented and satisfied life?

Psalm 37:4

_____
_____
_____
_____
_____

Isaiah 58:10-11

_____
_____
_____
_____
_____

John 6:35

_____

_____

_____

_____

_____

_____

Cultivate Creativity

Whenever people combine the word "creativity" and "sex," a lot of minds immediately think of things that are kinky or perverse. But that's not the case at all! Creativity is healthy in your marriage relationship. Creativity helps increase the fascination and intrigue. It sparks the excitement of young love. And it keeps you growing closer and more intimate.

One of the keys to cultivating creativity is sharing not just your needs but also your desires. Read 1 Corinthians 7:2-5. Make a list of the four specific instructions given in this passage.

1. _____

2. _____

3. _____

4. _____

In what ways do these instructions help couples guard against sexual sin?

_____

_____

_____

_____

_____

_____

_____

When is the last time you shared a sexual need with your spouse?
What was the response?

_____

_____

_____

_____

_____

_____

_____

_____

What can you do to foster an atmosphere where both you and your
spouse feel comfortable talking about sex more often?

_____

_____

_____

_____

_____

_____

_____

_____

"Creativity takes a whole lot of work, but the payoff is huge. We believe that creativity and excellence honor God and inspire people. . . .
Ever seem like you are drifting? That loss of romance and that drifting
are the result of ruts. The reason the romance seemed so exciting at
first is because it was new and fresh" (p. 146).

Cultivating creativity requires great communication. Sitting down
and talking about the issues and topics in your life—especially your sex
life—can go a long way toward creating an atmosphere of trust and
comfort where creativity can thrive.

Here are some great discussion questions for you and your spouse
to tackle one on one. While these questions aren't appropriate for
group discussion, they can help cultivate creativity in your marriage!

Do you prefer to be on the top or the bottom?

_____

_____

_____

_____

_____

What position do you prefer?

_____

_____

_____

_____

_____

Complete the following sentence: *I like it best when you* . . .

_____

_____

_____

_____

_____

Complete the following sentence: *I like it least when you* . . .

_____

_____

_____

_____

_____

How many times a week would you like to have sex? How many times a week would it be reasonable for us to have sex?

_____

_____

_____

_____

_____

_____

Is there anything I do that makes you feel uncomfortable?

_____

_____

_____

_____

_____

_____

Is there anything I say—even in passing conversation—that makes you feel unattractive?

_____

_____

_____

_____

_____

Is there anything new that you'd like me to do to prepare the room?

_____

_____

_____

_____

_____

Is there anything new that you'd like to try sexually?

_____

_____

_____

_____

_____

As you cultivate creativity in your sexual relationship, nurturing honor and security in your relationship becomes all the more important. That means not sharing with anyone anything that your spouse doesn't feel comfortable sharing with anyone else. Remember that what goes on inside the bedroom is between you and your spouse. If you take any details or stories outside the bedroom, you need to get permission first.

Hebrews 13:4 says, "Honor marriage, and guard the sacredness of sexual intimacy between wife and husband" (*THE MESSAGE*). Are there any ways in which you feel the trust in your sexual relationship needs to be renewed? If so, prayerfully discuss this issue with God and your spouse, and then list some areas that need work.

_____

_____

_____

_____

_____

_____

Taking It with You

Sometimes couples lose the fascination and curiosity that once brought them together. The good news is that you can renew the wonder and excitement. As you honor one another and build security in your marriage, you naturally create an atmosphere of intimacy, which leads to great sex.

Honor ➞ Security ➞ Intimacy ➞ *Sex*

By verbally affirming one another and serving one another, you naturally raise the temperature in your relationship. By developing realistic sexpectations and cultivating creativity, you can't help but have great sex. In the next session, you'll discover the spiritual dimensions of sex and how your personal relationship with God affects your relationship with your spouse. To prepare for the next session, read chapter 10 in *The Language of Sex*.

Putting It into Practice

Choose at least one of these suggested activities to complete over the next week. Consider sharing with your friends or small-group members the impact it has on you and your relationship with your spouse.

1. Write a Scripture-Based Love Note to Your Spouse
When was the last time you wrote a love note to your spouse, just letting him or her know your thoughts and feelings? In order to spice it up a little, take the following Scripture from Song of Songs 4:1-15 and rewrite the passage in your own words for your spouse. You may even want to select some special paper or pens to craft your love note.

2. Write an Open Invitation to Your Spouse
Write your spouse a card that reads, "Something we have never tried before but that I am open to is . . ." Leave it blank and allow him or her to fill it out and return it to you. Give your spouse some time. (Keys to remember: Both of you must be comfortable with it and it cannot violate Scripture.)

The Spiritual Dimensions of Sex

Chapter 10 in *The Language of Sex*

Couples who have been happily married for many years often describe a tendency to think alike and respond alike. At times, one person will know what the other is thinking without a word having been said. How does this happen? In part it comes from the familiarity of living life together, but it's also an expression of the holy mystery that happens when two married people share their lives together. At the core of the holy union of marriage is commitment—a commitment to each other for life.

The act of marriage is not just a physical and legal act but also a spiritual act. In the same way, sex is not just a physical or emotional act but also a spiritual act. Sex is a spiritual experience as two become one. It's a mystery but also something incredibly beautiful.

Spiritual commitment deepens the level of connection between a man and woman and therefore deepens the level of great sex. When we are secure in a right relationship with God, we are better able to love and be loved. We are free to be ourselves and to give ourselves. It all goes back to that equation:

Honor ➝ Security ➝ Intimacy ➝ *Sex*

When we commit ourselves to God and ask Him to transform us and make us into who we are really created to be—people filled with love, compassion, grace, strength and hope, fully committed to Christ— then He equips us with everything we each need to be a great spouse and lover. We learn how to honor our spouse as we learn to honor God. We learn to offer security to our spouse as we discover the security found in God. And as we learn to take time to pray, study God's Word and fellowship with other followers of Jesus, we discover what an intimate relationship with God looks like and we are better prepared to have an intimate relationship with our spouse. God wants to be with us every step of the way!

Participating as a couple in simple spiritual activities—prayer, reading the Bible and worshiping through music—adds yet another vibrant dimension to your relationship. As honor, security and intimacy grow, you'll find yourself having a more satisfactory relationship and sex life.

For Starters

Why do you think God designed sex as more than just a physical act?

_____

_____

_____

_____

_____

_____

What activities or disciplines help you connect with God? What prevents you from doing those activities or disciplines more often?

_____

_____

_____

_____

_____

_____

Do you find that your life and relationship are affected when you take time to read the Bible and pray? Explain. What happens when you don't take time to read the Bible and pray?

_____

_____

_____

_____

_____

_____

_____

Introduction to DVD

"Gina Ogden, a sex therapist researching at Harvard University, is the author of the book *Women Who Love Sex*. She is currently studying the connection between women, sex and spirituality. She says, 'The key to deeper satisfaction is connecting sexuality to spirituality.'[1] In other words, sexuality and spirituality go together. The most sexually fulfilled women were also the most spiritual women. When you miss the spiritual dimension that's naturally a part of sex, you miss out on part of the pleasure" (p. 163).

A great marriage is founded on honor and security, which leads to intimacy and results in great sex. In this fourth session, we'll explore the spiritual dimensions of sex and the four spiritual commitments that can transform your relationship. Let's watch as Gary and Ted introduce this subject.

Discussion and Study

The Four Spiritual Commitments
There are four spiritual commitments you can make that can have an impact on your marriage, relationships and life. Let's look at each one.

1. I will remove the expectation that my mate will meet all of my needs.
While you may not consciously expect your mate to meet all of your
needs, there may be little ways—even unspoken ones—in which you expect your mate to meet your needs. Maybe it's a need for conversation,
friendship, encouragement, courage or hope. All of those are valid needs,
but they create an atmosphere of codependence whenever you look at
one person to fulfill all of a given need.

"Too often, couples believe that their happiness is based on each
other. But our real happiness, our true joy, is based on our individual
relationship with God. Couples often say they need help with their
marriage, as if they don't have problems as individuals—it's just when
they get together that their problems and sin manifest themselves.
They blame their marriage for the issues—but the issues were in place
before the marriage" (p. 172).

God is not only the One who wants to fulfill all of your needs—He's
also the only One who can!

On the chart below, draw lines connecting the Scripture references with
the matching promise of God.

Scripture	Promise of God
Psalm 18:2	"The Lord gives sight to the blind, . . . lifts up those who are bowed down, [and] . . . loves the righteous."
Psalm 49:15	The Lord is our "rock, . . . fortress, . . . deliverer; . . . shield and . . . stronghold."
Psalm 73:26	"The Lord is . . . a refuge in times of trouble. cares for those who trust him."
Psalm 146:8	The Lord will redeem our lives and take us to Himself.
Nahum 1:7	God is enough. He "is the strength of [our] heart and [our] portion forever."

In the Sermon on the Mount, Jesus makes it clear that He does not want us to fear anything. Instead, we are to turn to God to meet all of our needs. Read Matthew 6:25-34. What worries are listed in this passage?

_____

_____

_____

_____

_____

_____

Of those worries listed above, are there any that you are particularly susceptible to?

_____

_____

_____

_____

_____

_____

Are there any worries that become areas of tension or disagreement in your marriage?

_____

_____

_____

_____

_____

_____

What instruction is provided in Matthew 6:33 as the antidote to worry?

_____

_____

_____

_____

_____

_____

Above all, God wants you to seek Him for everything! When you turn first to God with your needs and desires, He naturally becomes the One you depend on. He becomes a source of hope and strength for whatever you're going to face. And that takes the burden off of your spouse. Your spouse no longer has to try to carry a load that was designed for God alone.

2. I will make every effort to seek my fulfillment from God.
There are so many places in life where you can seek fulfillment from someone or something other than God. You can easily become distracted or busy and miss the opportunity to connect with God each day. This is demonstrated clearly in two parables in the book of Matthew.

Read Matthew 13:18-23. According to this passage, what undermines the seeds yielding the crop?

_____

_____

_____

_____

_____

_____

_____

_____

Read Matthew 22:1-5. In this passage, what response did the guests have to the invitation to the wedding feast?

_____

_____

_____

_____

_____

_____

_____

In both passages, we discover that it's impossible to be fully fruit-ful in our lives apart from God. He is the source of our life and redemp-tion. He is the One who extends a grand invitation to each of us—to be in relationship with Him. But we must seek our fulfillment from God and avoid those things that distract and choke the God-life out of us.

"The real secret to creating more hunger in your spouse if he or she does not believe in God is by letting your mate see a model of someone becoming more like God without any signs of criticism from you about his or her behavior. Most people haven't seen a person who has hidden God's words within his or her heart and thus been led to godly transformation, or who has submitted to the Holy Spirit and thus has received amazing power to both love and bless others. When these two habits are formed in you, your unbelieving mate can discover the reality of God and His ways. When you're not being critical, your spouse gets to witness a real live model of God's transforming power in action" (p. 168).

3. I will take 100 percent responsibility for my spiritual journey.

It's amazing how easy it is to assign the responsibility of your spiritual journey to someone else. You may think it's up to your parents, teach-ers, coaches, pastors or youth leaders to lead you into a closer relation-ship with God; but at the end of the day, it's really up to you. You are the one who is responsible for studying the Bible, praying, spending time in fellowship with other believers and growing in your faith. You can't do it alone—you need others to accompany you on the journey—but you can't blame others for your own shortcomings or laziness.

"Take responsibility for your own—and only your own—spiritual journey. You must identify your own need for Christ to fill the empti-ness in your life. This first step begins a journey, not a race. Too often we like to package life change in a nice and neat 6- or 13-week Bible study. This has created a faulty idea that life change happens fast. I believe real life change is typically slow. I like to think in terms of years, not weeks or months. This alone should encourage a couple not to think their marriage will be perfect or on track after a few sessions with a pastor or counselor. Give it time" (p. 171).

In the book of Genesis, we read of the first time spiritual blame was cast. Read Genesis 3:1-13. In this passage, who was blamed for the poor decisions?

_____

_____

_____

_____

_____

Why do you think the natural response for Adam and Eve was to blame someone else?

_____

_____

_____

_____

_____

Who do you tend to blame when something goes wrong in your life? Your spiritual journey?

_____

_____

_____

_____

_____

Read 1 Samuel 25. In what ways did Abigail take 100 percent responsibility for her spiritual and personal journey? What was her reward?

_____

_____

_____

_____

_____

Real change begins on the inside. It's not about fixing yourself up on the outside to make yourself presentable to God. It doesn't work that way. It's about changing from the inside out, which is something only God can do. He is the only One who can change a human heart. How freeing is that? Not just for you, but also for your spouse! You no longer have to manipulate, control, conquer and subdue your mate. You can let God be God.

4. I will make God, not my mate, the center of my life.
God should be the center of your life! That may mean that you have some work to do on your heart in order to make Him the center. There are so many distractions, so much busyness and so many things from the past that are a result of sin and fear that can hold you back. Yet the Bible gives you a key to making God the center of your life. It's found in Psalm 119:11: "I have hidden [God's] word in my heart that I might not sin against [God]." When you begin replacing the messages of the world with the messages of Christ through Scripture, not only does your heart change, but also your priorities.

According to Luke 5:32, what hope is there for those who struggle to make God the center of their lives?

_____

_____

_____

_____

_____

_____

According to Colossians 3:16, what are some practical ways you can hide God's Word in your heart?

_____

_____

_____

_____

_____

_____

_____

"When we practice simple spiritual disciplines like prayer, worship and fellowship, we get filled up and the peace of Christ rules in our hearts. When our focus is on God, then our spouses naturally get to enjoy the overflow" (p. 172).

When God is the center of your life, people can't help but notice the difference—including your spouse. First Peter 3:14-15 says, "But even if you should suffer what is right, you are blessed. 'Do not fear what they fear; do not frightened.' But in your hearts set apart Christ as Lord. Always be prepared to give an answer to everyone who asks you to give the reason for the hope that you have."

What do you think Peter means by his instruction "In your hearts set apart Christ as Lord"?

_____
_____
_____
_____
_____

What would you say is the reason "for the hope that you have"? Write a few sentences describing what God has done in your life.

_____
_____
_____
_____
_____
_____

Taking It with You

Sex is not just a physical act. Sex is an emotional, relational and *spiritual* act. When you and your spouse are in an intimate relationship with God, you are better equipped and prepared to be in an intimate relationship with one another. It all goes back to the equation:

Honor → Security → Intimacy → *Sex*

When you are growing in your relationship with God, you naturally attract others to grow in their relationship with God, too. That includes your spouse. In the next session, you'll discover how to resolve conflict and guard your marriage. To prepare, read chapters 11 and 12 in *The Language of Sex.*

Putting It into Practice

Choose at least one of these suggested activities to complete over the next week. Consider sharing with your friends or small-group members the impact it has on you and your relationship with your spouse.

1. Hide the Word in Your Heart

This week commit to memorize at least three Scriptures. Several are suggested below, but feel free to choose your own.

> God is our refuge and strength, an ever-present help in trouble. Therefore we will not fear, though the earth gives way and the mountains fall into the heart of the sea, though its waters roar and foam and the mountains quake with their surging (Psalm 46:1-3).

> I have told you these things, so that in me you may have peace. In this world you will have trouble. But take heart! I have overcome the world (John 16:33).

> Let the word of Christ dwell in you richly as you teach and admonish one another with all wisdom, and as you sing psalms, hymns and spiritual songs with gratitude in your hearts to God (Colossians 3:16).

2. Take a Spiritual Inventory

Reflect on the following questions prayerfully. Spend time responding to each one.

Is there anything right now that is holding you back or distracting you from your relationship with God?

_____

_____

_____

_____

_____

What changes do you need to make in your life to be more intentional about growing in your relationship with Christ?

_____

_____

_____

_____

_____

Are there any areas of sin that you're flirting with? What do you need to do to remove the temptation from your life?

_____

_____

_____

_____

_____

Is there anyone who you are holding unforgiveness toward in your home? Workplace? Church?

_____

_____

_____

_____

_____

Where have you seen God most active in your life? What are you doing to nurture that area of your life?

_____

_____

_____

_____

_____

_____

3. Commit to Connect Spiritually with Your Spouse

If you don't already connect spiritually with your spouse on a regular basis, talk about developing a new plan to connect one on one. Here are some ideas to get you started:

- Pray together each night before you go to bed.
- Pray together each morning when you first wake up.
- Pray for your spouse every day!
- Commit to read one chapter of the Bible together each day.
- Read the same spiritual book. Make time to discuss what you're learning.
- Watch a spiritually themed movie together and discuss it afterward.
- Place Bibles throughout the house in easily accessible areas.
- Use a prayer book together on a regular basis.
- Join a small group or Bible study.
- Volunteer to serve others.
- Sign up for an overseas missions trip.
- Visit popular Christian websites and print out articles to discuss.
- Read sections of a Bible promises book together.
- Study the Bible together.

Note
1. Gina Ogden, quoted in "Sex and Spirituality," Oprah.com, 2007. http://www.oprah.com/relationships/relationships_content.jhtml?contentId=con_20020916_sexspirit.xml&section=Sex&subsection=Sex (accessed November 2007).

Resolving Conflict and Guarding Your Marriage

Chapters 11–12 in *The Language of Sex*

Have you ever seen the movie *Dirty Harry* with Clint Eastwood? Do you remember the scene where the bad guy is getting away, and Clint Eastwood jumps on the hood of the car? No matter what, he is sticking to that car. He—or rather, his stunt double—is flying all over the place, but he manages to stay on. That scene is a portrait of the heart God has for marriage. He wants us to stick through the thick and thin—for better and for worse.

Years ago, when two people got married, the guests were considered part of the ceremony. They were invited not only to enjoy the celebration, but also to be part of the accountability structure. They were witnesses to the covenant of marriage that the bride and groom were making. They were committed to supporting the marriage and helping the bride and groom stay married for a lifetime. Today, when I (Ted) perform marriages, I'm quick to remind the attendants and the attendees of the important role that they play. I remind the best man that he is not just a best man but also a best friend. That means he is to stand by the groom and support the marriage. I remind the maid of honor that she has a crucial role, too, to support the marriage. I remind both the best man and the maid of honor that when times get tough in the marriage relationship, both of them have an opportunity to jump in and encourage the bride and groom to fight for and protect their marriage. And I remind those attending the ceremony that they also play an important role, supporting and encouraging the couple.

Sooner or later, conflict arises in every marriage. But when you base your relationship on commitment, then you've pledged to work through the conflict and find a resolution. Sometimes that isn't easy. There have been plenty of times I have been frustrated with my wife, but because of the commitment in our relationship, I know I've got to work through it. As we learn how to forgive and seek reconciliation, we develop the skills we need for good conflict resolution. The question for every couple isn't *When will conflict arise?*, but rather *How will you handle it when it does?*

Conflict resolution isn't the only skill you need to develop in a healthy marriage. You also need to learn how to guard and protect your relationship with your spouse. That means being proactive against the predators that can try to undermine your marriage and commitment to your spouse.

In this session, we're going to explore healthy ways to resolve conflict and to keep the security and honor that you've built into your marriage. In addition, we're going to look at the predators that can try to attack your marriage and how you can defend yourself from them.

For Starters

When was the last time you encountered a conflict with your spouse? What was the issue of the conflict? Was there a deeper issue behind the conflict?

_____

_____

_____

_____

_____

What kinds of things can weaken or undermine a marriage?

_____

_____

_____

_____

_____

_____

_____

_____

_____

What are you doing right now to guard your marriage from outside forces that may try to weaken or undermine your relationship?

_____

_____

_____

_____

_____

_____

_____

_____

_____

Introduction to DVD

Every marriage has conflict. The question is, *How do you and your spouse respond when conflict arises?* When you develop healthy ways to resolve conflict, then you protect the honor and security that naturally make your relationship thrive. And when you proactively guard your marriage from predators, then you're better able to have the marriage and sex life you've always wanted. In this fifth session, you'll discover what the Bible says about resolving conflict and how to guard your marriage wisely. Let's watch as Gary and Ted introduce you to these ideas.

Discussion and Study

The commitment that you make to your spouse on your wedding day is one of the most important commitments you'll ever make. It becomes the foundation not just for your marriage but also for your family.

My (Ted's) daughter Corynn, age three, still doesn't know how to handle it when I'm affectionate with my wife in the kitchen. I'll be hugging and kissing my wife, and Corynn will yell, "What are you doing, Daddy? Leave her alone!"

I'll explain, "I'm showing your mommy how much I love her!"

As soon as she hears those words, she wants to get in the middle of it! So my wife and I will start hugging and kissing our daughter until she can't stop giggling. We love our time with her, and from the big smile on her face, we know she loves her time with us!

Sometimes people are tempted to let go of the commitment they made on their wedding day. They see divorce as an easy out and even buy into the lie that the children will be better off if the parents separate. But that is a lie! Children are happiest when their parents are together creating security for them.

When a husband and wife divorce, who is hurt by the breakup? Make a list of people who are hurt.

_____

_____

_____

_____

_____

The key to all conflict resolution—no matter how significant or trivial the conflict—is being rooted in a relationship with God. You can learn lots of relational skills, but apart from a relationship with God, lasting change is difficult if not impossible. The good news is that no matter how hostile a relationship, resolution can be found if both parties are willing to work through the conflict and to change. It does take time, but God can work miracles.

Read Matthew 12:25. According to this Scripture, what is the effect of unresolved conflict in a relationship?

_____

_____

_____

_____

_____

_____

_____

Intruders of Intimacy

There are four intruders of intimacy that appear any time conflict goes unresolved. The first intruder is *escalation*. A conflict may be small and easily dismissed, but when escalation enters, the conflict grows disproportionately large. Something small like the fact the dirty clothes landed near the hamper rather than in it suddenly becomes highly important and significant—even when it's really not.

"Escalation is an intruder that sneaks in quietly but quickly. Many times, escalation shows up because we have bottled up our feelings and emotions. In a single moment, something happens and, *snap*—we let it all out. Escalation works much like a volcano. You never know when it is going to erupt, and you usually cannot control the flow" (p. 181).

When an issue appears—no matter how small—your emotions feed on similar situations that happened in the past. The unresolved anger sparks your response. Before you know it, the issue has grown disproportionately large.

What do the following Scriptures prescribe to resolve anger?

Mark 11:25

_____

_____

_____

_____

_____

Ephesians 4:25-27

_____

_____

_____

_____

_____

Ephesians 4:31-32

_____

_____

_____

_____

_____

James 1:19-21

_____

_____

_____

_____

_____

The second intruder is *harsh language*. If anger is left unresolved, a conflict can quickly escalate and, before you know it, unkind and cruel words can be said. Sadly, there are some things that are difficult if not impossible to take back. That's why it's so important to be aware and to defend yourself from using harsh language.

What do the following Scriptures prescribe to avoid harsh language?

Proverbs 15:1

_____

_____

_____

_____

_____

1 Timothy 5:1

_____

_____

_____

_____

_____

Jude 14-16

_____

_____

_____

_____

_____

The third intruder is _retreat_. This one may seem innocent enough. When conflict arises, you may be tempted to shut down, run away or use some other means to avoid the situation. But that doesn't really resolve anything—in fact, it actually opens the door to other intruders like escalation and harsh language. Instead, you should be ready to face conflict with prayer, grace and love, knowing that the sooner you deal with a situation, the healthier the relationship will be.

"Retreat is used by those who just want the conflict to be over; they don't even need resolution to anything. A person who retreats will do or say anything just to make the conflict stop. And all of the unresolved issues are still on the table" (p. 182).

Read Jonah 1:1-3. What did the Lord instruct Jonah to do? How did Jonah respond?

_____

_____

_____

_____

_____

_____

All of us have different forms of retreat. We may choose the silent treatment, busyness or simply giving in. Jonah's form of retreat was to take a boat to a distant land. What are some of your favorite forms of retreat?

_____

_____

_____

_____

_____

_____

Read Jonah 1:4-17. In His great love for the people of Nineveh and Jonah, the Lord would simply not allow Jonah to retreat. How did the Lord prevent Jonah from running away?

_____

_____

_____

_____

_____

How can your spouse or those around you help you not to retreat?

_____

_____

_____

_____

_____

How can you help your spouse and those around you not to retreat?

_____

_____

_____

_____

_____

The fourth intruder is *assumption*. You allow assumptions to intrude on your relationships when you don't take time to talk or communicate about issues. Instead, you begin filling in the blanks of what the other person is thinking or doing. This is dangerous ground, because it allows conflict not only to arise but to go unresolved. Once assumptions creep into a relationship, it's only a matter of time before the other intruders—escalation, harsh language and retreat—find their way in, too.

Read Luke 10:38-42. What assumptions did Martha make about Mary? What assumptions did Mary make about Martha?

_____

_____

_____

_____

_____

_____

Which intruders do you see demonstrated in this passage?

_____

_____

_____

_____

_____

_____

How did Jesus respond? How is Jesus' answer a model response for us?

_____

_____

_____

_____

_____

_____

What do the following Scriptures prescribe to resolve conflict?

Matthew 5:44

_____
_____
_____
_____
_____

Matthew 18:21-22

_____
_____
_____
_____
_____

Colossians 3:13

_____
_____
_____
_____
_____

1 Peter 3:9-10

_____
_____
_____
_____

"Nowhere in the Bible do we find that arguing, screaming or the silent treatment provides any sort of solution for conflict. Those things simply don't work. God has not empowered you to change your spouse's heart. He has kept all that power to Himself. Instead, He invites you to love, serve and reflect Himself to the person you married" (pp. 187-188).

The Five Dreaded Sexual Predators

In addition to avoiding the intruders in your relationship, it's important to be aware of the predators that will try to attack and undermine your marriage commitment. These predators want you to break your marriage vows and succumb to lust, an affair and even divorce.

The first predator is the *vacuum of intimacy*. When you and your spouse are not intimately connected, the door to looking for fulfillment in other places from other people is opened. The second predator is *fantasy*. Whenever you allow your imagination to begin walking—let alone running—wild about someone other than your spouse, this predator begins to take over your mind. Once you begin imagining yourself with someone else, it usually isn't too long before the third predator enters in: the *intentional encounter*. You may begin looking for moments at church, at work or in your neighborhood to run into this particular other person. Once this happens, you can't help but allow the fourth predator in: the *expression*. You begin expressing your thoughts and feelings to this other person; and before you know it, the fifth and final predator has gripped you: *acting out*. Now you've crossed every line and broken your marriage vows.

The Bible makes it clear that while we will all face temptation and intruders in our relationship, we do not face them alone. God is not only with us, but He wants also to protect us.

Read Matthew 4:1-11. In this passage, what did Jesus use to guard Himself from temptation?

_____

_____

_____

_____

_____

_____

_____

What do these verses prescribe to guard against lust and temptation?

Job 31:1

_____

_____

_____

_____

_____

Proverbs 6:20-24

_____

_____

_____

_____

_____

Proverbs 6:25-26

_____

_____

_____

_____

_____

Matthew 6:13

_____

_____

_____

_____

_____

Because it is a truth that both men and women can fall into immorality, we all need to recognize the destroyers and learn how to prevent a fall. It's like Paul says: "We are not unaware of his [the devil's] schemes" (2 Corinthians 2:11); and Peter corroborates: "The devil prowls around like a roaring lion looking for someone to devour"

(1 Peter 5:8). While the devil can't take your soul because you are secure with Jesus, he can get you to the point where you are disqualified, distracted and lost.

In Genesis 39, we read about Joseph and his dealings with Potiphar's wife. He could have had an intimate encounter with her, but instead he refused. Read Genesis 39:6-12. What did Joseph do to guard and protect his purity?

_____

_____

_____

_____

_____

_____

_____

Are there any predators currently attacking your marriage? What steps do you need to take, like Joseph, to get away?

_____

_____

_____

_____

_____

_____

_____

_____

Taking It with You

Conflict is inevitable, but you can develop skills to resolve conflict with grace and love. As you learn to resolve conflict in your marriage relationship, you preserve honor and security and intimacy. As your marriage relationship deepens, you still have to guard against the intruders and predators that will try to undermine your marriage. But it's all worth it!

Your relationship is worth preserving and protecting. In the next session, we'll explore some of the biggest and most common questions regarding marriage, relationships and sex; and we'll provide practical, biblically based answers. To prepare, read the appendix in *The Language of Sex*.

Putting It into Practice

Choose at least one of these suggested activities to complete over the next week. Consider sharing with your friends or small-group members the impact it has on you and your relationship with your spouse.

1. Plan a Quarterly Marriage Realignment (QMR)

In the busyness of life, it's easy to allow issues to remain unresolved. Whether the issues are about parenting, bills, planning, sexual interest or household duties, some issues can go untouched. That's why it's important to have a regular meeting time and place where it's safe for you and your spouse to discuss issues. Amy and I (Ted) call our meetings Quarterly Marriage Realignments (QMR). About four times a year, we sit down and talk about everything that's on our hearts, minds and schedules. We delve into the issues behind the issues, and at the end of our time together—which can last from 30 minutes to several hours—we are more connected and compassionate toward each other.

Sometime this week, plan a QMR with your spouse. Give each other a few days' notice so that you can prayerfully think about issues and details that may have been swept under the rug in the rush of life. Open the time with prayer. Commit to really listen to each other, speak works thoughtfully and in love, and know that the goal of this time is to strengthen your relationship.

2. Ask God to Reveal Any Intruders or Predators in Your Life

Throughout this session, intruders (escalation, harsh words, retreat and assumption) as well as predators (the vacuum of intimacy, fantasy, the intentional encounter, the expression and acting out) were explored. Take a few moments to prayerfully consider each of these areas.

Are there any intruders that you are particularly prone to? Are there any predators in your life that you need to deal with? If so, you may need some help. Consider joining an accountability group or seeking a counselor grounded in the Bible. It's never too late to begin protecting and fighting for your marriage.

3. Memorize Three Scriptures to Protect Your Mind from Lust

Hide the following three Scriptures in your heart this week. Say them aloud a few times throughout each day.

No temptation has seized you except what is common to man. And God is faithful; he will not let you be tempted beyond what you can bear. But when you are tempted, he will also provide a way out so that you can stand up under it (1 Corinthians 10:13).

What is more, I consider everything a loss compared to the surpassing greatness of knowing Christ Jesus my Lord, for whose sake I have lost all things. I consider them rubbish, that I may gain Christ and be found in him, not having a righteousness of my own that comes from the law, but that which is through faith in Christ—the righteousness that comes from God and is by faith (Philippians 3:8-9).

Finally, brothers, whatever is true, whatever is noble, whatever is right, whatever is pure, whatever is lovely, whatever is admirable—if anything is excellent or praiseworthy—think about such things (Philippians 4:8).

Answers to the Biggies

The Appendix in *The Language of Sex*

When it comes to marriage, relationships and sex, there are a lot of great questions out there! One of the most common questions we're asked is about submission between a husband and wife. The question arises because of the following passage in Ephesians 5:

> Wives submit to your husbands as to the Lord. For the husband is the head of the wife as Christ is the head of the church, his body, of which he is the Savior. Now as the church submits to Christ, so also wives should submit to their husbands in everything.
>
> Husbands, love your wives, just as Christ loved the church and gave himself up for her to make her holy, cleansing her by the washing with water through the word, and to present her to himself as a radiant church, without stain or wrinkle or any blemish, but holy and blameless. In this same way, husbands ought to love their wives as their own bodies. He who loves his wife loves himself. After all, no one ever hated his own body, but he feeds and cares for it, just as Christ does the church—for we are members of his body. "For this reason a man will leave his father and mother and be united to his wife, and the two will become one flesh." This is a profound mystery—but I am talking about Christ and the church. However, each one of you also must love his wife as he loves himself, and the wife must respect her husband (vv. 22-32).

Wives ask why they're instructed to submit to their husbands. They read the first part of the passage without reading the rest. Yes, wives are commanded to submit to their husbands, but the husbands are commanded to *die*—they are to give up their lives—for their wives. It's much like the question about who sacrifices more for a breakfast of ham and eggs . . . the pig or the chicken? It's the pig—he has to die. The chicken just lays the egg. So it goes in marriage.

But the question of submission isn't the only question we're commonly asked. We also get asked about the different sexual desires of men and women. We try to explain the differences using the following word picture:

If you are going to enjoy a nice meal at night from a Crock-Pot, there is nothing better than baby back ribs with Sweet Baby Ray's Sauce cooked for 12 hours. Having become a fan of great barbecue, I've learned that there's no way I could come home at 5:30 P.M., place the ingredients in the pot and expect to have slow-simmered, mouth-watering baby back ribs by 6:00 P.M. In the same way, women take time to simmer sexually. They aren't turned on instantly. Men, however, are ready to go at a moment's notice. They're like fast food or a microwave. One of the best ways to understand the sexual differences between men and women is by recognizing the time each takes to heat up.

In this final session, we're going to examine some of the common questions that arise when it comes to marriage, relationships and sex.

For Starters Discussion Questions

If you could ask a doctor one medical question regarding sex, what would you want to ask?

_____

_____

_____

_____

_____

_____

_____

_____

_____

If you could ask a counselor one question regarding sex or your marriage, what would you want to ask?

_____

_____

_____

_____

_____

_____

_____

Where do you tend to go when you have questions about sex? Marriage? Relationships?

_____

_____

_____

_____

_____

_____

_____

Introduction to DVD

We all have questions about marriage, relationships and sex. Sometimes it's hard to know where to go for answers. The Bible is meant to be our foundation and source, but there are also a lot of outside resources, including counselors, pastors, doctors and friends, to help us along the way. In this final session, we'll explore some of the biggie questions about marriage and sex and what the Bible has to say on these issues. Let's watch Gary and Ted introduce this subject.

Discussion and Study

One of the questions that we often get is, *How can I assist my spouse on his/her spiritual journey?* The key to this is found in Ephesians 5. Read Ephesians 5:1-2. What instruction is given with regard to how we should live? We are to "be imitators of God"—as His children—and we are to "live a life of love." We are to lay down our life for our spouse.

What does "lay down your life for your spouse" mean?

_____

_____

_____

_____

_____

_____

_____

_____

_____

What impact does serving and loving your spouse have on your spouse's attitude? On your spouse's response to you? On your spiritual journey?

_____

_____

_____

_____

_____

_____

_____

_____

According to Romans 8:29, the goal of our lives is to be conformed to the likeness of Jesus. That is a process, not a one-time or overnight event. And those around us—including our spouse—get to see the transformation firsthand. One of the best things you can do for your spouse's spiritual journey is to begin praying. Instead of talking about your faith, begin living it through service, love, kindness and good deeds. Lay down your own life. Ask God to conform you to the image of His Son. Before you know it, you'll discover that spiritual growth is more contagious than you could have imagined!

Other questions we often receive circle around the theme of dissatisfaction with sex. Either the wife or the husband is not content—they want more. And while the desire should be expressed, it should also be examined. How much is really enough? If I compare myself to an empty glass that waits to be filled, how much will it take to be filled? I might start believing that if I meet the right person, that person will provide some water, and my glass will start to fill up a little. We'll get married, which adds a little more water. Then we'll have hot sex, which fills my glass to the brim. Or does it? If we have a child, the glass will be full. Or maybe if we have more children, the glass will be full. Or maybe if we pay off our house or get out of debt or retire or get an extra week of vacation, the glass will be full.

Do you get the picture?

If you're dissatisfied in your marriage, sex life or relationships, then it's time to take an inward look at the root cause. What's filling you up? Where is your contentment coming from? How much is really enough?

According to the following passages, what is the secret to contentment?

Psalm 37:7

_____

_____

_____

_____

_____

Psalm 37:16

_____

_____

_____

_____

_____

_____

Proverbs 16:8

_____

_____

_____

_____

_____

_____

Thankfulness is a wonderful antidote to discontentment. When you are appreciative of what you have—rather than unhappy about what you don't have—you discover a joy and satisfaction that you didn't know was possible.

On the chart below, identify *who* demonstrated thankfulness and gratitude and *how* they demonstrated it.

Bible passage	Person showing thanks	How gratitude was demonstrated
1 Chronicles 29:10-13		
Daniel 2:17-23		
Luke 2:36-38		

One of the all-time most popular questions we receive is in regard to pornography. Sexual immorality of all kinds—including pornography—is one of the greatest destroyers of your spiritual growth and marriage. You don't want the images of sexual interactions of anyone but your spouse in mind when you're having sex. Think about it: When you are making love to your spouse and the lights are out and your eyes are closed, you don't want your spouse imagining someone else! When you introduce pornography into your marriage, you're introducing an addiction that will undermine your relationship.

The Bible is very clear regarding sexual immorality. In the following passages, what instruction does the Bible give regarding sexual immorality?

1 Corinthians 6:15

_____
_____
_____
_____
_____
_____

1 Corinthians 6:18-20

_____
_____
_____
_____
_____

1 Thessalonians 4:3

_____
_____
_____
_____
_____

Hebrews 13:4

_____

_____

_____

_____

_____

_____

Another common question we get is about sexual mistakes made in the past. People who have made such mistakes want to know how they can move on. The good news is that God "is faithful and just and will forgive our sins and purify us from all unrighteousness" (1 John 1:9). That means that no matter what you've done in the past, nothing is beyond His redeeming power.

In the following verses, what promises are found regarding past sin, forgiveness and redemption?

Psalm 103:12

_____

_____

_____

_____

_____

_____

Proverbs 28:13

_____

_____

_____

_____

_____

_____

Isaiah 1:18

_____

_____

_____

_____

_____

_____

_____

Isaiah 43:25

_____

_____

_____

_____

_____

_____

2 Corinthians 5:17

_____

_____

_____

_____

_____

_____

Ephesians 1:5-7

_____

_____

_____

_____

_____

_____

One question that people don't ask often enough is, *Why are sex and marriage so great?* The answer is because God designed us to enjoy marriage as we celebrate and delight in one another—physically, emotionally, relationally and spiritually.

Taking It with You

There are a lot of questions about marriage, relationships and sex, and you don't have to struggle to answer them alone! The Bible is an incredible source of wisdom and insight. In addition, pastors, Christian counselors and others can come alongside you to help you find the answers you need. As you continue to build honor and security in your marriage, you'll find yourself more connected to your spouse each day. As intimacy flourishes, so will the sex, as you enjoy the fullness of the pleasures God intended for married couples.

Putting It into Practice

Choose at least one of these suggested activities to complete over the next week. Consider sharing with your friends or small-group members the impact it has on you and your relationship with your spouse.

1. Make a List of Your Own Questions

Maybe you have a few questions about sex, your marriage or your relationships. Commit to finding the answers from a healthy source—a doctor, counselor, trustworthy friend or mentor—this week. You may even want to email us your questions. You can visit the Smalley Relationship Center online by going to www.garysmalley.com or to www.tedcunningham.com.

2. Talk to Your Kids About Sex

You may have been putting off talking to your kids about sex. You may have already had an awkward discussion or been asked a few embarrassing questions. But it's never too early to develop a game plan to talk to your kids about sex and sexuality. If you don't address the issue, then the odds are that someone who knows a lot less than you do will do it for you— maybe in the locker room at school. How can you talk to your kids about sex?

Tom Holladay, a pastor from Saddleback Church in California, provides some wonderful insights on how to teach our kids about sex. He quotes Deuteronomy 6:6-7: "These commandments that I give to you today are to be upon your hearts. Impress them on your children. Talk about them when you sit at home and when you walk along the road, when you lie down and when you get up."

God's commands include instructions regarding sex. Holladay points out that *two* of the Ten Commandments are about sex! The secret to talking to your kids about sex is not making it a one-time talk but an ongoing conversation in which they feel comfortable coming to you to ask questions and find out the truth. Sometime this week, sit down and talk to your spouse about how your family can address issues of sexuality more comfortably as an ongoing dialogue instead of a one-time birds-and-bees talk. Depending on the age of your children, go ahead and begin the dialogue.

3. Give Thanks to God

One of the ways to honor and glorify God is through worship. Read Psalm 100. Spend a few minutes thanking God for the way He made your spouse. Then spend a few minutes thanking God for the way He made you. Finally, spend a few minutes thanking God for bringing you two together, for your marriage and for your future together. Ask God to continue to use you and your spouse to bless and encourage others.

Leader's Guide

Session 1
The Foundations of Honor and Security
Chapters 1–3 in *The Language of Sex*

During this session, couples will explore the issues of honor and security and the vital role they play in your marriage and sex life.

For Starters

When you think of the word "honor," what comes to mind? Answers will vary, but words that come to mind may include "respect," "attach worth to" or "treat extremely well."

In what practical ways do you honor your spouse? Answers will vary, but this icebreaker question is meant to highlight the kind and good things each person does for his or her spouse.

What are the ways your spouse feels most honored? Are there any differences between the ways you think your spouse feels most honored and the ways your spouse actually feels honored? If so, explain. Answers will vary, but this question is designed to help spouses communicate with one another and discover what really makes each one feel most honored and appreciated. Spouses might just be surprised by what they learn.

Discussion and Study

Honor is the foundation of every great relationship, including our relationship with God. We are called and created to honor God. In the following verses, in what way is honor displayed to God?

- Psalm 29:2: Honor is displayed by giving the Lord the glory due His name, which is honoring Him and knowing His worth. Honor is also given through worship, or ascribing worth. The phrase "splendor of his holiness" implies that the psalmist has his eyes on God—the psalmist is focusing on God.

- Psalm 107:32: Honor is displayed through publicly speaking well of God. Among people of all ages—including the elders— God is honored.

- Isaiah 25:1: Honor is displayed through verbal affirmation and acknowledging the things God has done. The writer also acknowledges specific attributes of God—including faithfulness—which are appreciated.

List five specific ways in which you honor God in your own life. Answers will vary, but people honor God by obeying His commands, worshiping, serving and giving out of a grateful heart. They honor God by spending time with Him, praying, listening and seeking Him. They honor God when they fix their attention and heart on God. They honor God when they love others.

Take a second look at the Scriptures that prescribe honor to God. As you reflect on the Scriptures, what insights do you have on how you can honor your spouse?

- Psalm 29:2: Just as the Lord should be given "the glory due his name," with an appreciative heart we can acknowledge our spouse for all he or she does. Sometimes the simplest thank-you and acknowledgement of services goes a long way toward encouraging our spouse. The psalmist writes, "Worship the Lord in the splendor of his holiness." In other words, the psalmist has fixed his eyes on God. We also need to take time to fix our eyes on our love and let our spouse know how much he or she is appreciated and adored. We need to look into their eyes and show appreciation for who they are and who God has made them to be.

- Psalm 107:32: Just as the Lord can be exalted "in the assembly of the people," we can make sure the words that we speak of our spouse in public are always filled with grace, love and kindness. We can look for opportunities to let others know about our spouse's good works, character and kindness. When we say good things about our spouse away from our spouse's hearing, the words usually get back to our spouse—and they're reminded again of the extent of our love and appreciation.

- Isaiah 25:1: Just as the psalmist acknowledges, "You are my God," we, too, can take time to acknowledge the role of our spouse in our life by verbally affirming, "You are the love of my life," "You are my best friend," "You are my treasure" and "You are my delight." When we verbally affirm our spouse in specific ways, we can literally change the atmosphere of the relationship.

Read Genesis 2:18. Notice that God didn't just make "a helper" but "a suitable helper for him." Why do you think God took so much care in His design of a spouse for Adam? Answers will vary, but God specifically designed someone who was just perfect for Adam. If God took so much time and delicate care with creation, think how much time and delicate care He took with designing Eve for Adam! When God brings a man and woman together, He creates a beautiful portrait.

What foxes are running through your relationship with your spouse right now? Are there any foxes that you need to catch and remove from your marriage? A lot of foxes can eat away at a relationship if they're not caught. These include anger, bitterness, unforgiveness, busyness, and lack of communication. Foxes can manifest themselves in issues—money, sex, in-laws or even parenting styles—when a couple touches on an issue but never finds a way to resolve it. It's important to catch foxes early and often, lest they eat away at honor and security, which should be foundational in every marriage.

Read Malachi 2:10-16. Why do you think God is so opposed to divorce? God opposes divorce because it hurts all parties involved. Not only do the spouses hurt emotionally, spiritually, mentally and even financially, but also the long-term impact on the children of divorce is immeasurable. In addition, divorce undermines a person's testimony as a follower of God: Forgiveness, grace and reconciliation are talked about but not lived out in families and relationships. God is opposed to divorce, but He loves the divorced person and extends grace and restoration.

Marriage is representative of something greater than just the union between a man and a woman. It's also representative of God's relationship with His people, the Church. According to the passages below, what can we learn about God's desire for a relationship with us?

- Isaiah 62:5: God rejoices over us with the kind of joy felt by a bride and groom.

- 2 Corinthians 11:2: God is jealous over us with a holy jealousy. Christ is our husband—a holy relationship—in which we are to keep ourselves pure.

- Revelation 19:7: This passage alludes to the wedding feast that is to come. The bride, the Church, has made herself ready.

- Revelation 21:2: The Holy City, the new Jerusalem, is compared to "a bride beautifully dressed for her husband."

Reflecting on your own marriage, are there any unhealthy boundaries that are undermining your relationship? Answers will vary, but unhealthy boundaries can develop anytime an unhealthy proportion of time, money and energy are given to something. Unhealthy boundaries can develop in schedules, free time, workplaces, families, friendships and other relationships.

Session 2
Celebrate Differences and Discover Communication
Chapters 4–6 in *The Language of Sex*

During this session, couples will celebrate their natural differences as well as learn to take their communication to the next level to foster intimacy in their marriage relationship.

For Starters
In the space below, list three ways that you and your spouse are alike. These can include gifts, talents, weaknesses, interests, passions, visions, dreams and hopes. Answers will vary, but the responses should remind each couple of the common interests, passions and dreams they share.

Now list three ways you and your spouse are different. Answers will vary, but the differences mentioned should be celebrated. People have differences because they bring unique talents, gifts and strengths to relationships.

In what ways do those differences complement each other? In what ways do those differences help add balance to each of your lives? This question is the core of the starter discussions for this session. So often we tend to look at differences as dividing points instead of connecting points of how we can live better, healthier and more balanced lives together.

Discussion and Study
Read Psalm 139:14-18. Make a list of all the things God has done for us and knows about us. God creates and makes each one of us. We are "fearfully and wonderfully made" (v. 14). He knows everything about us. He ordained our days for us. He thinks of us often and in more wonderful ways that we can imagine. God is always with us. He does not leave us or forsake us.

God doesn't just know everything about us—He wants us to know Him. In the passages below, what promises are given to those who seek God, who desire an intimate relationship with Him?

- Deuteronomy 4:29: If we seek God with all of our heart and soul, then we will find Him.

- 2 Chronicles 7:14: If God's people humble themselves, pray, repent and seek God, then He will hear from heaven, forgive their sins and heal their land.

- Psalm 9:10: Those who seek God are never forsaken.

When you reflect on your marriage relationship so far, how have you seen your level of intimacy with your spouse increase? On a scale of 1 to 10, how much do you feel that you know about your spouse? On a scale of 1 to 10, how much do you feel that your spouse knows about you? Answers will vary, but this question is designed to highlight the fact that there's always more to learn about your spouse. You'll simply never know everything—there's always more to discover. One of the reasons for this is that God is always changing and shaping us. As Christians, we are not stagnant—we are constantly growing and becoming more like Jesus as we pursue a relationship with Him.

What kind of activities tend to build intimacy in your marriage? Answers may vary, but activities may include taking walks, playing sports, shopping, serving others, volunteering, or other activities. Usually, spending time together and talking fosters intimacy.

What kinds of activities tend to undermine intimacy in your marriage? Conflict, anger, unforgiveness, bitterness and busyness can all undermine intimacy in a marriage.

How does your spouse's response to this quiz differ from your own? In what areas do you tend to think alike? Answers will vary, but this question is designed to help married couples understand each other better.

1. Men tend to want to discover and express facts, and women tend to express intuition and their emotions. Do you agree or disagree that this statement is true in your marriage? Explain. How can you make this an area of greater agreement and appreciation between you and your spouse? Answers will vary, but this question is designed to allow each couple to discover whether or not these key differences apply in their marriage. The hope is that this question will lead to better understanding, communication and intimacy within the relationship.

2. The majority of men are looking for solutions, while most women are looking for compassion, empathy and understanding. Do you agree or disagree that this statement is true in your marriage? Explain. How can you make this an area of greater agreement and appreciation between you and your spouse? Answers will vary, but this question is designed to allow each couple to discover whether or not these key differences apply in their marriage. The hope is that this question will lead to better understanding, communication and intimacy within the relationship.

3. Most men tend to be more objective, while most women tend to be more personal. Do you agree or disagree that this statement is true in your marriage? Explain. How can you make this an area of greater agreement and appreciation between you and your spouse? Answers will vary, but this question is designed to allow each couple to discover whether or not these key differences apply in their marriage. The hope is that this question will lead to better understanding, communication and intimacy within the couple's relationship.

4. A lot of men can separate who they are from their surroundings, whereas the home is an extension of most women. Do you agree or disagree that this statement is true in your marriage? Explain. How can you make this an area of greater agreement and appreciation between you and your spouse? Answers will vary, but this question is designed to allow each couple to discover whether or not these key differences apply in their marriage. The hope is that this question will lead to better understanding, communication and intimacy within the relationship.

5. Men tend to focus on the basics, while women tend to focus on details that make up the big picture. Do you agree or disagree that this statement is true in your marriage? Explain. How can you make this an area of greater agreement and appreciation between you and your spouse? Answers will vary, but this question is designed to allow each couple to discover whether or not these key differences apply in their marriage. The hope is that this question will lead to better understanding, communication and intimacy within the relationship.

Read Matthew 14:22-31, Matthew 26:69-75 and John 6:60-69. Reflecting on these passages, how would you describe Peter? How was God able to use Peter? Peter was naturally impulsive. He was always ready for an adventure and, undoubtedly, at times he was the life of the party. Peter was also easily distracted and not always dependable. Yet Peter was one of Jesus' closest disciples and experienced redemption. Through his time with Christ, he became a "rock" (Matthew 16:18) and an amazing evangelist.

Read Acts 16:36-37, Acts 20:25-37 and 2 Timothy 4:7-8. Reflecting on these passages, how would you describe Paul? How was God able to use Paul? Paul was strong, outspoken and a born leader. He desired justice and was not ashamed of the gospel. Paul was bold. He was an encourager and was inspirational. Even when he knew that his own death was near, he still remained faithful. He was hard working and committed to spreading the gospel as far as possible. God used Paul to help evangelize and build the Church.

You may not realize just how important your words are in your marriage and other relationships. Read Proverbs 18:21. Just how much power is there in your words? According to this Scripture, there is the power of life and death in your words. Now that's a lot of power!

The Bible provides practical and valuable insight on how to develop strong communication skills. Look up the passages below. What can you learn from the following Scriptures to enhance your communication skills?

- Exodus 20:16: Good communication means not speaking ill of anyone.

- Proverbs 15:28: Good communication takes time. Think and pause before offering an answer.

- Proverbs 16:32: Good communication means controlling your temper and learning to be patient.

- Proverbs 18:13: Good communication means taking time to really listen before responding.

- Matthew 5:33-37: Good communication means keeping your word.

- 1 Corinthians 13:1: Good communication means grounding your words in love.

How does miscommunication undermine your relationships? What is the cost to others—God, family, friends and coworkers—when you don't communicate or listen well? Miscommunication causes unnecessary tension, anger and confusion. Miscommunication can lead to distrust and broken relationships. The cost is tremendous in relationships and lives.

How does learning how to communicate well improve your relationships? Your marriage? Learning how to communicate well can revolutionize relationships as love, grace, compassion and understanding pour from a person's speech. Good communication leads to stronger, healthier, long-lasting relationships that are fun and honoring to God.

Session 3
Foreplay, Intercourse and Creativity
Chapters 7–9 in *The Language of Sex*

During this session, couples will explore foundational issues related to sex. They will discuss such topics as the importance of verbal affirmation, healthy expectations and the cultivation of creativity.

For Starters

How has the romance in your relationship changed since you were first married?
Answers will vary, but this question is designed to highlight the fact
that romance—and the definition of romance for each of us—changes
during the course of a marriage.

*What kinds of activities, words or interactions cultivate romance, affection and
fascination in your relationship?* Spending time together and common activities often increase the level of romance, affection and fascination.
But it's important to be intentional about one another. A couple can
do the same activity and either be connected or disconnected based on
how much positive interaction they enjoy.

*What prevents you from pursuing those activities, exchanging those words and en-
joying those interactions more often?* Busyness, schedules, children, work,
house repairs and other daily chores can prevent a couple from pursuing those activities.

Discussion and Study

*List five nonsexual activities that help prepare you or make you desire sex with
your spouse:* Answers will vary, but acts of service top the list for activities that prepare many women for sex. Nothing says "Sex" like vacuum-
ing or taking care of the kids for many women. Taking a shower, caring
for personal hygiene, clean sheets on the bed, love notes or calls throughout the day can all help prepare desire.

In each of these passages, what verbal affirmation did God offer Joshua?

- Joshua 1:6: "Be strong and courageous."

- Joshua 1:7: "Be strong and very courageous."

- Joshua 1:9: "Be strong and courageous. Do not be terrified;
  do not be discouraged."

- Joshua 1:18: "Be strong and courageous!"

Why do you think Joshua needed to hear the verbal affirmation more than once? Answers will vary, but maybe Joshua didn't allow the affirming words to sink into his heart the first time. Maybe—like many of us—he needed to hear those words a second, third and even fourth time.

If Joshua needed to hear verbal affirmation from God multiple times, how much more do you and your spouse need verbal affirmation? Most of us need more verbal affirmation than we realize! We need to be reminded regularly of what is kind, good, true and beautiful. We need to be encouraged regularly.

Why do you think it's so important to affirm each other verbally before and after intercourse? Sex is incredibly intimate and requires extreme vulnerability. Affirmation before and after sex can make one feel assured that honor and security are part of the relationship.

"The top thing a woman wants from a man is gentleness. The top thing a man wants from a woman is responsiveness" (p. 111). In what ways do you agree with this statement? In what ways do you disagree? Answers will vary, but generally this is true for most couples.

All of us have insecurities. What are some of the more intimate insecurities that you have when it comes to sex? Share your response with your spouse. Answers will vary, but many spouses struggle with insecurities such as body image, size, duration or performance.

In the space below, list the expectations you have for yourself. Answers will vary from generalities to specifics. Some people expect that they or everyone else will always be on time, always be kind or always be clean and organized. They may expect perfection, success or equality. They may expect to meet their goals—or even the goals of others.

In the space below, list the expectations you have for your spouse. Answers will vary, but this question is designed to highlight the fact that we all place expectations on our spouse—whether we realize it or not. Some of those expectations may be healthy, but others may not be.

Are your expectations realistic and healthy? Take a moment and pray. Ask God if there are any changes that you need to make in your expectations. List the necessary changes. Answers will vary, but expectations that undermine a relationship are usually not healthy. Expectations that create repeated disappointment, anger, frustration or bitterness should be prayerfully evaluated.

In what ways are grace and redemption demonstrated in the following verses?

- Proverbs 4:18: We are reminded that we have not arrived at perfection, but that the light of righteousness is constantly growing brighter as we continue our Christian walk.

- 2 Corinthians 3:18: We are reminded that each of us is being transformed into God's likeness. We have an ever-increasing glory, which comes from God.

- 2 Thessalonians 1:3: We see an attitude of gratefulness displayed. We are reminded that faith and love are constantly increasing.

As Christians, we are called by God to be content in all circumstances. We are to find our joy and satisfaction in the One who will not leave us or forsake us. What do the following verses prescribe for a contented and satisfied life?

- Psalm 37:4: Delight in God, and He will give us whatever we desire.

- Isaiah 58:10-11: When we serve, defend and bless others, then we ourselves are served, defended and blessed by the Lord. He satisfies all of our needs and gives us strength.

- John 6:35: Establish a relationship with Jesus. He is the One who satisfies us like no other.

One of the keys to cultivating creativity is sharing not just your needs but also your desires. Read 1 Corinthians 7:2-5. Make a list of the four specific instructions given in this passage.

1. Each person should be married to one other person of the opposite sex.
2. Each person should fulfill his or her marital duty.
3. Each person's body is not his or her own (which includes love and respect).
4. Each person should not deprive the other except for the reason of prayer.

In what ways do these instructions help couples guard against sexual sin? They instruct us that sex should be a regular part of a healthy marriage. Sex should not be ignored or deprived or used as a reward; it should be mutually enjoyed. This helps close the door on sexual temptation.

When is the last time you shared a sexual need with your spouse? What was the response? Answers will vary, but this question is designed to allow couples to talk about their comfort levels of communicating about sex.

What can you do to foster an atmosphere where both you and your spouse feel comfortable talking about sex more often? Couples should realize that they need to be intentional about taking time to talk about sex—not just as a joke or prelude to intercourse—but a real heart-to-heart discussion. They need to listen to each other. They need to respond graciously and honestly. The words each spouse speaks need to be seasoned with kindness and love.

Session 4
The Spiritual Dimensions of Sex
Chapter 10 in *The Language of Sex*

During this session, couples will explore the spiritual dimensions of sex. They will explore such topics as the importance of a relationship with God and assuming 100 percent responsibility for their own individual spiritual journey.

For Starters

Why do you think God designed sex as more than just a physical act? Answers will vary, but sex is an amazing gift with many dimensions. It's a gift that we're meant to unwrap for a lifetime with our spouse.

What activities or disciplines help you connect with God? What prevents you from doing those activities or disciplines more often? Answers will vary but prayer, Bible study, worship, solitude, silence, spiritual retreats and other disciplines can help people connect with God. Busyness can prevent people from connecting with God.

Do you find that your life and relationship are affected when you take time to read the Bible and pray? Explain. What happens when you don't take time to read the Bible and pray? Answers will vary, but most people experience a change in attitude and perspective that affects their day in a great way. Not taking the time to read the Bible and pray also affects a person's attitude and perspective—but not in the best way.

Discussion and Study
1. *I will remove the expectation that my mate will meet all of my needs.*

On the chart below, draw lines connecting the Scriptures with the promises of God.

Scripture	Promise of God
Psalm 18:2	"The LORD gives sight to the blind, . . . lifts up those who are bowed down, [and] . . . loves the righteous."
Psalm 49:15	The Lord is our "rock, . . . fortress, . . . deliverer; . . . shield and . . . stronghold."
Psalm 73:26	"The LORD is . . . a refuge in times of trouble. He cares for those who trust him."
Psalm 146:8	The Lord will redeem our lives and take us to Himself.
Nahum 1:7	God is enough. He "is the strength of [our] heart and [our] portion forever."

In the Sermon on the Mount, Jesus makes it clear that He does not want us to fear anything. Instead, we are to turn to God to meet all of our needs. Read Matthew 6:25-34. What worries are listed in this passage? The worries include what we will eat, drink or wear, and the future.

Of those worries listed above, are there any that you are particularly susceptible to? Answers will vary. Each person has different areas where he or she is more tempted to worry about.

Are there any worries that become areas of tension or disagreement in your marriage? Answers will vary.

What instruction is provided in Matthew 6:33 as an antidote to worry? We are to seek God and His kingdom and righteousness. We are to place God as the top priority.

2. I will make every effort to seek my fulfillment from God.

Read Matthew 13:18-23. According to this passage, what undermines the seeds yielding the crop? Lack of roots, some trouble or persecution, worries about life, and the deceitfulness of riches can all prevent good growth.

Read Matthew 22:1-5. In this passage, what response did the guests have to the invitation to the wedding feast? They refused to come. "They paid no attention and went off—one to his field, another to his business" (v. 5).

3. I will take 100 percent responsibility for my spiritual journey.

In the book of Genesis, we read of the first time spiritual blame was cast. Read Genesis 3:1-13. According to this passage, who was blamed for the poor decisions? Adam blamed Eve, and Eve blamed the serpent.

Why do you think the natural response for Adam and Eve was to blame someone else? None of us wants to take responsibility for our actions or sins. Like Adam and Eve, we all want to hide.

Who do you tend to blame when something goes wrong in your life? Your spiritual journey? Answers will vary, but blame may be placed on parents, church, pastor, spiritual leaders, boss or spouse. Some people may also blame themselves or God.

Read 1 Samuel 25. In what ways did Abigail take 100 percent responsibility for her spiritual and personal journey? What was her reward? Abigail recognized her husband's foolishness and did what was right—preserving her own life as well as her family. In the end, her husband died and she was married to David, which placed her in the lineage of Jesus.

4. I will make God, not my mate, the center of my life.

According to Luke 5:32, what hope is there for those who struggle to make God the center of their lives? Jesus is the hope. He came to call the sinners, not the righteous. So even if God isn't the center of your life, He can still become the center.

According to Colossians 3:16, what are some practical ways we can hide God's Word in our hearts? We can teach and encourage each other with Scripture. We can sing Scripture songs, hymns and worship songs. We can look for opportunities to offer thanks to God.

What do you think Peter means by his instruction "In your hearts set apart Christ as Lord"? Answers will vary, but his instruction means that every person is to make Christ the center of his or her life. That's something that produces change from the inside out.

What would you say is the reason "for the hope that you have"? Write a few sentences describing what God has done in your life. Answers will vary, but participants should be encouraged to share their reasons for the hope they have for people who don't know Jesus yet.

Session 5
Resolving Conflict and Guarding
Your Marriage
Chapters 11–12 in *The Language of Sex*

During this session, couples will discover how to resolve conflict as well as guard their marriage from intruders and predators that may try to undermine it.

For Starters
When was the last time you encountered a conflict with your spouse? What was the issue of the conflict? Was there a deeper issue behind the conflict? Answers will vary, but the point of this question is to highlight the fact that often in a conflict, there are deeper issues going on. A couple may argue about money, but the core issue may be security or freedom.

What kinds of things can weaken or undermine a marriage? Unresolved conflict, lack of communication, unforgiveness, harsh words, lying, cheating, stealing and bitterness are just a few of the many things that can weaken or undermine a marriage.

What are you doing right now to guard your marriage from outside forces that may try to weaken or undermine your relationship? Making wise choices, guarding our eyes, healthy communication and prayer are just a few of the many ways marriage can be guarded.

Discussion and Study
When a husband and wife divorce, who is hurt by the breakup? Make a list of people hurt. Answers will vary, but the husband and wife are hurt. The children are often devastated. The neighbors, friends and surrounding community are affected, too. When a couple divorces, there's a sense of loss to everyone who knows them. Every relationship is affected by one or both spouses.

Read Matthew 12:25. According to this Scripture, what is the effect of unresolved conflict in a relationship? The effect of unresolved conflict in a relationship is ruin and collapse.

What do the following Scriptures prescribe to resolve anger?

- Mark 11:25: Pray for those you are angry with, and as you pray, choose to forgive them.

- Ephesians 4:25-27: Always speak the truth. Though you experience anger, don't let it go unresolved, even for a day.

- Ephesians 4:31-32: Let your response be tempered. Never shout angrily or say cruel things. Don't let your anger manifest itself in your actions. Be loving. Be kind. Forgive, just as God forgave you.

- James 1:19-21: Listen carefully to what the other person is saying, think before you say anything, and don't lose your temper. Study God's Word, and hide it in your heart.

What do the following Scriptures prescribe to avoid harsh language?

- Proverbs 15:1: Answer with gentleness.

- 1 Timothy 5:1: Instead of speaking harshly, choose to encourage and exhort others.

- Jude 14-16: Trust that the Lord will respond and take care of the words spoken harshly against you. And take care that you do not respond in such a harsh way yourself.

Read Jonah 1:1-3. What did the Lord instruct Jonah to do? How did Jonah respond? The Lord instructed Jonah to go to Nineveh. Instead, Jonah got on board a boat to another land.

All of us have different forms of retreat. We may choose the silent treatment, busyness or simply giving in. Jonah's form of retreat was a boat to a distant land. What are some of your favorite forms of retreat? Answers will vary, but in addition to the forms of retreat listed above, many people choose retreat by avoiding the issues, not speaking up, and agreeing to disagree on all issues.

Read Jonah 1:4-17. In His great love for the people of Nineveh and Jonah, the Lord would simply not allow Jonah to retreat. How did the Lord prevent Jonah from running away? God sent a storm so violent that the safety of the ship that Jonah was on was threatened. When the sailors threw lots to find out whose fault it was, Jonah was discovered. Once Jonah was thrown overboard, the Lord sent a giant fish to swallow him—both as a source of protection and to provide an opportunity to take time to reconsider.

How can your spouse or those around you help you not to retreat? Answers will vary, but one of the best ways is to lovingly remind the person that he or she is shutting down. Sometimes a warm hug or listening ear can go a long way toward helping a person not to shut down.

How can you help your spouse and those around you not to retreat? Answers will vary, but one of the best ways is to lovingly remind the person or people that they're shutting down and that you care too much about them to let them do that. Sometimes a warm hug or listening ear can go a long way to helping others avoid shutting down.

Read Luke 10:38-42. What assumptions do you imagine Martha made about Mary? What assumptions do you imagine Mary made about Martha? Answers will vary, but we can imagine Martha thought Mary was simply not doing anything. Maybe Martha thought Mary was shirking her responsibility. Mary may have assumed Martha had everything under control and really didn't need her. She may have lost track of time or thought her earlier preparations were enough to get her sister through. She may have even assumed that someone else was in the kitchen helping Martha.

Which intruders do you see demonstrated in this passage? Martha's words to Jesus demonstrate escalation, harsh language and assumption. From what we read in this passage, Martha did not really retreat.

How did Jesus respond? How is Jesus' answer a model response for all of us? Jesus responded firmly, but His words were seasoned with love, grace and truth. He did not allow the conflict to escalate. He did not use hard language. He did not retreat. And He did not allow any assumptions to remain. He was straightforward but gracious.

What do the following Scriptures prescribe to resolve conflict?

- Matthew 5:44: Pray for your enemies or those you have conflict with.

- Matthew 18:21-22: Forgive as many times as it takes. Don't place a limit on the forgiveness you offer.

- Colossians 3:13: We are to forgive others, but the source of that forgiveness is remembering that God also forgave us.

- 1 Peter 3:9-10: Do not do wrong to repay a wrong or return insult for insult. Instead, bless those who you are in conflict with.

Read Matthew 4:1-11. In this passage, what did Jesus use to guard Himself from temptation? He used the Word of God. Hiding the Word in our hearts protects us from temptation.

What do the following verses prescribe to guard against lust and temptation?

- Job 31:1: Promise not to look lustfully at anyone.

- Proverbs 6:20-24: Remember the words of your father and mother. Keep solid, good teaching close to your heart.

- Proverbs 6:25-26: Do not lust after beauty. Be careful what you fix your eyes on. Stay away from adulterers and prostitutes.

- Matthew 6:13: We can ask God to protect us from temptation and keep us from the evil one. This is part of the prayer Jesus instructed His disciples to pray. We can pray this every day and even throughout the day.

In Genesis 39, we read of Joseph and his dealings with Potiphar's wife. He could have had an intimate encounter with her, but instead he refused. Read Genesis 39:6-12. What did Joseph do to guard and protect his purity? He refused the advances of Potiphar's wife. He did not give in. He kept his focus on his job duties and God. When things became particularly heated, Joseph physically removed himself from the situation and ran away.

Are there any predators that are currently attacking your marriage? What steps do you need to take, like Joseph, to get away? Answers may vary, but cutting off a relationship, changing a job or even talking to a counselor to get help may be needed.

Session 6
Answers to the Biggies
The Appendix in *The Language of Sex*

During this final session, some of the common questions that arise when it comes to marriage, relationships and sex will be discussed.

For Starters
If you could ask a doctor one medical question regarding sex, what would you want to ask? Answers will vary, but questions may concern dryness, discomfort, frequency, pain or other physical issues.

If you could ask a counselor one question regarding sex or your marriage, what would you want to ask? Answers will vary, but people often have questions regarding their own expectations or what others have told them is normal regarding sex.

Where do you tend to go when you have questions about sex? Marriage? Relationships? Answers will vary, but sources include friends, counselors, books, magazines and the Internet, to name just a few.

Discussion and Study

What does "lay down your life for your spouse" mean? It means to place your spouse's interests, desires and priorities above your own.

What impact does serving and loving your spouse have on their attitude? On your spouse's response to you? On your spiritual journey? Answers will vary, but generally, serving and loving your spouse has a positive impact on the spouse.

According to the following passages, what is the secret to contentment?

- Psalm 37:7: Waiting patiently and avoiding fretting help foster contentment.

- Psalm 37:16: Contentment comes when we realize that a little with righteousness is better than a lot with the wicked.

- Proverbs 16:8: Contentment comes when we realize that righteousness is our greatest gain.

On the chart below, identify who *demonstrated thankfulness and gratitude and* how *they demonstrated it.*

Bible passage	Person showing thanks	How gratitude was demonstrated
1 Chronicles 29:10-13	David	Public praise to God
Daniel 2:17-23	Daniel	Public prayer and praise to God
Luke 2:36-38	Anna	Public thanks to God and speaking about Jesus

The Bible is very clear regarding sexual immorality. In the following passages, what instruction does the Bible give regarding sexual immorality?

- 1 Corinthians 6:15: Sexual immorality, including prostitution, is clearly forbidden.

- 1 Corinthians 6:18-20: "Flee sexual immorality" (v. 18). We are to honor God with our beliefs.

- 1 Thessalonians 4:3: God's will is that sexual immorality should be avoided.

- Hebrews 13:4: The marriage and the marriage bed should be honored and kept pure. Adulterers and the sexually immoral will be judged by God.

In the following verses, what promises are found regarding past sin, forgiveness and redemption?

- Psalm 103:12: God takes our sins as far away from us as the west is from the east.

- Proverbs 28:13: Confessing and renouncing sin leads to mercy. Hiding our sins does not lead to prosperity.

- Isaiah 1:18: God can cleanse us of our sins. No stain of sin is beyond His power and redemption.

- Isaiah 43:25: God "blots out" sins and forgets them.

- 2 Corinthians 5:17: If we are "in Christ," we are new creations. All the old things are gone, and everything is made new.

- Ephesians 1:5-7: God "predestined us to be adopted" as sons and daughters through Jesus. Through Christ, we have redemption.